GLASGOW'S SPITFIRE

Glasgow Museums

We are grateful to all the pilots, 602 Squadron Museum, Dugald Cameron, Alan Carlaw, and Rolls Royce, who have kindly allowed us to reproduce their photographs. All efforts have been made to trace copyright holders, but if any have been inadvertently omitted, please notify the publisher.

Image page 18 courtesy of the Imperial War Museum, London, negative number CH 14810.
Images pages 19 and 76 © Dugald Cameron, reproduced by kind permission.
Images pages iii and 5 © Crown Copyright, reproduced with permission.
Back cover photograph © Ian Watson.

Edited by Alex Robertson, Dugald Cameron and Susan Pacitti

Designed and typeset by Trish Copson

Printed in Great Britain

Published 2003 by Glasgow Museums.

ISBN 0 902752 73 1

The restoration and display of the Spitfire is a joint project between Glasgow Museums and The National Museums of Scotland, and was generously supported and funded by the Scottish Executive.

Glasgow Museums would like to thank 602 Museums Association, Rolls Royce, A.H. Bowman, Professor Dugald Cameron OBE, Alan Carlaw, J.A. Forrest AE, Malcolm Houston, DM Jack AE, JA Johnston DFC, Air Vice Marshal AVR Johnstone CB DFC AE DL, CH MacLean AE DL and Alex Richardson for their generous assistance in compiling this publication.

Front cover photograph shows 602 Squadron at their first annual camp, RAF Woodvale near Southport, July 1947, in front of LA198.
Back row, left to right: Flight Lieutenant Yuille, Flying Officer Reid (killed during that camp), Flying Officer McWilliams, Flight Lieutenant Hume, Flight Lieutenant Jackson, Flying Officer Richardson and Flying Officer Robinson.
Middle row, left to right: Flight Lieutenant Cunliffe Regular Adjutant, Flight Lieutenant Dunlop Urie, Squadron Leader Robinson Commanding Officer, Flight Lieutenant Jack and Flight Lieutenant 'Doc' Stewart, Medical Officer.
Front row, left to right: Sergeant Reid, Sergeant MacGuire, Sergeant Lake, Flight Sergeant Forrest, Sergeant Melling and Sergeant Mitchell.

The Squadron Standard was granted by His Majesty King George VI and promulgated on 27 March 1952.
It was presented by The Duke of Hamilton and Brandon at the Squadron Headquarters,
49 Coplaw Street, Glasgow, on 3 March 1957, and was laid up in Glasgow Cathedral on the same day.

No. 602 (City of Glasgow) Squadron
Royal Auxiliary Air Force

Battle Honours
Home Defence 1940–1945 Battle of Britain 1940
Fortress Europe 1940–1944 Channel and North Sea 1940–1943
Dieppe France and Germany 1944–1945 Normandy 1944

The dedication of LA198 as RAF Leuchars gate guardian, 1986.

Contents

Spitfire LA198 in the Museum of Transport, Glasgow, 2003.

This book tells the story of Supermarine Spitfire LA198, her short flying career as told through the eyes of the men of 602 (City of Glasgow) Squadron, and her subsequent restoration.

From the beginning, this has been a joint project between Glasgow Museums and the National Museums of Scotland, and it was to The Museum of Flight at East Fortune that LA198 was delivered in April 1998. Procedures were then adopted to ensure that interested members of the public could view the restoration as it progressed.

In December 1998, a Senior Restorer, Derek Macphail, was employed. He quickly set about employing two technicians, James Neil and Joanne Macraild. Documentation of a project such as this is vital, as even the removal of the smallest screw, nut or bolt must be recorded. A policy was implemented immediately so that every item removed from LA198 was given a red tag that was dated and initialled, ensuring that every part was accounted for. In this way, a full history of the restoration has been accumulated for posterity.

As suspected, the aeroplane was in worse condition than we had hoped. More rust and corrosion were found on each part that was removed. Many of the parts of the aeroplane were missing; for instance, it had no wheels and roughly only half of the engine. Our restorers spent a lot of time tracking down original parts that are now very rare.

Over the life of this project staff have come and gone. Joanne left us in 1999 to be replaced by Kyle Meldrum. In 2000, Derek left us and the project management was taken over by Barry Ratcliffe of The National Museums of Scotland. Ray Baird joined us as the paint specialist, and he has been ably advised by Professor Dugald Cameron so that the final colours are completely accurate. Finally, Robert Jarvis joined the team in 2001.

Our objective was to restore LA198 to the best possible condition and there can be no doubt that this has been achieved. We are very proud to be able to display this magnificent aeroplane as a symbol of Glasgow's achievements, an acknowledgement of the heroism of her people, and a reminder of her history.

There is no substitute for witness testimony, so we have included oral histories from the men of 602 Squadron relating to their experiences in Spitfires, and in LA198 specifically.

We are very grateful to the Scottish Executive for funding the Spitfire's restoration and returning it for display within Glasgow Museums. We would also like to thank Professor Dugald Cameron for his generous contributions, and most of all, the men of 602 (City of Glasgow) Squadron without whose co-operation this project would not have been possible.

Alex Robertson
Curator, Social History & Transport

It usually causes some surprise to learn that the 'father' of the Royal Flying Corps and, in effect, the Royal Air Force, was a Glaswegian – General Sir David Henderson, of the Glasgow engineering and shipbuilding family. He was a student at the University of Glasgow from 1877 to 1881 and a pupil of Lord Kelvin. Lord Trenchard, usually given the title, disclaimed it in Henderson's favour. Among Trenchard's very great achievements as Chief of the Air Staff from 1919 was the creation of the Auxiliary, later the Royal Auxiliary, Air Force – 'a corps d'elite, territorially based, like a crack cavalry regiment'.

No.602 (City of Glasgow) Squadron was the first to be formed, on 12th September 1925, at Renfrew Aerodrome with DH 9A and Avro 504K biplanes. In 1910, another Scot, Captain Bertram Dickson, had been among the first military men to understand what aeroplanes might do for the military.

Before the turn of the nineteenth century, when the City of Glasgow was at its zenith, Percy Pilcher, an assistant lecturer in naval architecture at Gilmorehill (Glasgow University) had successfully flown his hang gliders from the slopes of the Clyde near Cardross. Pilcher's flights in the summer of 1895 were the first truly 'piloted' ones in Great Britain. Neither Yorkshire baronet Sir George Cayley's 'boy'-carrying glider of 1849, nor that of his reluctant coachman in 1853, were actually 'flown' by their intrepid passengers. (However, Cayley is rightly recognized as laying down the basic principles of aeronautics.) Sadly, Pilcher died in October 1899 after an accident when demonstrating his fourth glider, the 'Hawk'. It had been built in Glasgow but not flown in Scotland, for he left to join Sir Hiram Maxim at Eynsford in Kent during the spring of 1896. He had, however, built a powered triplane, though his engine would not have been sufficiently powerful and he had not provided a satisfactory means of control, relying on bodyweight shift as in his gliders.

It was to be two brothers of genius, Orville and Wilbur Wright from Dayton, Ohio, who, starting just after Pilcher's death, succeeded in the quest which had attracted so many over the years – to fly like a bird. This they achieved at 10.35 a.m. Eastern Standard Time on 17th December 1903 at Kitty Hawk, North Carolina, USA. The necessities for successful piloted, sustained and controlled heavier-than-air flight were twofold, given a means of lift–a sufficiently light yet powerful power plant and crucially, a means of controlling the craft in three dimensions. The Wrights understood this from day one, and within four years had done the job by careful, systematic methodology and courage.

Glaswegians have played, and continue to play, a significant role in the development of aviation. Even before Pilcher, Joseph M. Kaufman, a Glasgow engineer, displayed a model of his idea for a flying machine at the Aeronautical Society of Great Britain's first exhibition at the Crystal Palace in 1868, the year in which Charles Rennie Mackintosh was born. The Barnwell brothers from Balfron in Stirlingshire, sons of the Managing

Director of the Fairfield Shipbuilding and Engineering Company where Pilcher had been an apprentice, were experimenting with flying machines at their home from 1905. They had studied at the Glasgow and West of Scotland Technical College, now the University of Strathclyde, and in January 1911 produced the first all-Scottish aeroplane to fly for more than half a mile, from Causwayhead to Bridge of Allan. (Blériot had flown the Channel a year and a half previously!)

Frank Barnwell, having graduated from Glasgow in naval architecture in 1905, went on to be both chief engineer and chief designer of the Bristol Aeroplane Company. His brother Harold became chief test pilot of Vickers, but was killed in 1917.

We should also remember other Scots who were boldly trying to fly in those early days, such as Preston Watson at Errol with his glider of 1903 and his subsequent powered aircraft from around 1906, latterly incorporating a novel means of lateral control in an attempt to provide an alternative to the Wrights' 'wing warping'.

Glasgow had seen its first demonstration of flying at Pollok Park in July 1910, James Radley doing the honours in a Blériot monoplane before participating in the great flying meeting at Lanark in August that year. On the Clyde, the great firm of Beardmores at Dalmuir built versions of the Sopwith 'Pup' and 'Camel' during World War I and also the large Handley Page V1500 bomber. It was tested at Inchinnan, Renfrewshire, where airships, including the famous R34, were made. They had also designed and built a number of prototype aircraft, and in the 1920s built the huge all-metal experimental 'Inflexible', as well as one of the two 'Inverness' flying boats using the Rohrbach system of all metal construction. In contrast, they also produced the tiny 'Wee Bee' and a remarkable fighter for the Latvian Government. Sadly, as the country's economic position deteriorated, the aircraft division, including its Reserve Flying School at Renfrew, was finally closed in 1929. David F. McIntyre from Govan, co-founder with the fourteenth Duke of Hamilton of Scottish Aviation Ltd at Prestwick, learnt to fly there. They were the first to fly over Mount Everest in 1933 and were successive commanding officers of 602 Squadron.

'A' flight, 602 Squadron, at Westhampnett 1940.

Scotland, in particular Glasgow and the West, has made a notable contribution to aviation, not least in the development of autogyros (an early form of helicopter) and helicopters. The Denny-Mumford machine was built in 1905 at Dumbarton and 'flew' intermittently up until the outbreak of the First World War. James G. Weir, pioneer flyer and brother of William, first Viscount Weir of Eastwood, and himself a greatly influential figure in political and industrial circles, became involved with the Spanish pioneer Juan de la Cierva. The firm of G&J Weir in Cathcart designed and built a series of prototype autogyros during the 1930s and then two helicopters in 1938 and 1939, the first before Sikorski in the USA. Along with other engineering and shipbuilding companies on the Clyde, Weirs had produced large numbers of aircraft during the First World War for the RFC (Royal Flying Corps) and RNAS (Royal Navy Air Squadrons). These autogyro interests are carried on today by Jim Montgomerie at Maybole, and in the Department of Aerospace Engineering at the University of Glasgow, who use a Montgomerie-Parsons autogyro for testing and research purposes.

Wars, and the prospect of war, act as a powerful, if dismal, stimulus to scientific and technological development. The City of Glasgow has produced much material and many warriors throughout the ages and in recent times still contributes notably to all three armed services.

The Vickers Supermarine Spitfire owes its creation to the genius of Reginald Mitchell and of Sir Henry Royce in airframe and powerplant terms respectively. Neither man lived to see it in operational service or its subsequent development by their colleagues throughout World War II. 'Glasgow's Spitfire', LA198, a late model Rolls-Royce Griffon-engined F.Mark 21, is a quite different aircraft from the early Merlin-powered machines, having almost twice the power and weight of the first machines. So different, in fact, that there was a proposal to call it the 'Victor'. Its return commemorates 602 Squadron, 'Glasgow's Own', and its great achievements in the Battle of Britain and throughout the war. It also reminds us of its re-formation at Abbotsinch after the war and the continuing commitment of Glasgow's 'weekend flyers'. 602 Squadron was equipped with Spitfire aircraft longer than any other unit – from 1939 to 1951. Along with 603, they went into battle on the 16th October 1939 when George Pinkerton and Archie McKellar shot down a German JU88 on a raid on shipping in the Firth of Forth. Pat Gifford of the Edinburgh squadron did likewise! Three other aircraft still exist that served with 602 – Spitfire 1a, R6915, LO-B in the Imperial War Museum, Lambeth, and LF Mark 16, TB382, LO-Z, flown operationally by weel kent BBC commentator Raymond Baxter during the latter stages of the war. A De Havilland Vampire jet, VT812, briefly served during 1953 and belongs to the RAF Museum.

We should also remember our other weekenders – No.2602 Light Anti-Aircraft Regiment Squadron which protected the airfields, and No.3602, a Fighter Control Unit, both based at RAF Bishopbriggs. And of course there was the Scottish Air Division of the Royal Navy Volunteer Reserve, the Fleet Air Arm's Nos.1830 and

1843 Squadrons and, effectively attached to the Army, 1967 Flight of No.666 Air Observation Post Squadron. Both were based at HMS Sanderling, Royal Naval Air Station Abbotsinch, now Glasgow International Airport.

In 1933 the Grey Douglas tartan was approved for officers' mess dress of the then two Scottish Auxiliary Squadrons, 602 and 603 (Glasgow and Edinburgh), and also used by their pipe bands. It was painted on the 602 Vampires and Meteors post-war and is now seen on the Grob Tutor aircraft of the Universities of Glasgow and Strathclyde Air Squadron – a reminder to the flyers of the future of an illustrious past. It is a happy coincidence that the centenary of powered flight was celebrated by the return of 'our' Spitfire, which will eventually hang in the refurbished Kelvingrove Art Gallery and Museum. There she will serve as a poignant memorial to those from this city and the West of Scotland whose courage and commitment helped to conquer the air and defend us. It is too, a splendid example of the great art of engineering, something we Glaswegians know very well.

No. 602 (City of Glasgow) Squadron Auxiliary Air Force

The official badge as approved by His Majesty King George VI in June 1937 and prepared by the Chester Herald at the College of Arms.

The badge is described in heraldic terms as follows: 'In front of a saltire azure fimbriated argent, a lion rampant gules' ('gules' being the heraldic term for red). The lion was adopted in view of the Squadron's association with Scotland; the saltire is indicative of the cross of St Andrew, being fimbriated to show it to be a white saltire on a blue ground. ('Fimbriated' is a heraldic term indicating a narrow border.)

The motto, 'Cave leonem cruciatum', translates as 'Beware the tormented lion'.

The badge is shown here set on the Grey Douglas tartan which was approved for the pipe band kilts and subsequently for officers' mess dress kilts. It was later used as the squadron markings in the post-war jet era.

Spitfire F.21 LA198 was ordered by the Ministry of Aircraft Production in May 1942, and was built at Vickers Armstrong's factory in South Marston, Wiltshire, in September 1944. Although earlier versions had used the Griffon engine, the Mark 21 was the first major design change to the Spitfire line since its birth. Departing from the original distinctive elliptical shape, it now had an entirely new wing which housed four 20mm Hispano cannons. The span was 36 feet 11 inches, and the aircraft was 32 feet 8 inches long, powered by a 2035 hp Rolls Royce Griffon 61 engine. It had a maximum speed of 449 mph at 25,000 feet and a service ceiling of 43,000 feet. Its normal range was 580 miles. Of the 20,351 Spitfires built, only 120 were Mark 21s, although some 3,000 were originally ordered.

LA198 was taken on charge by the Royal Air Force on 2 October 1944 at 33 MU (Maintenance Unit) Lyneham, Wiltshire, and stored there until 3 May 1945, when it was issued to the RAF's premier unit, No.1 (Fighter) Squadron, at RAF Coltishall, Norfolk, and allocated the code letters JX-C. When that squadron re-equipped with Meteor jets in October 1946, it was flown to RAF Cosford, Shropshire, for storage at 9 MU. It was issued to No. 602 (City of Glasgow) Squadron, Auxiliary Air Force, at RNAS Abbotsinch on 12 May 1947 where it was coded RAI-G. It suffered a minor flying accident on 25 October 1947 and was repaired by a working party from 63 MU Carluke, but a further accident on 11 July 1949 necessitated the aircraft's return to Vickers Armstrong for repair.

LA198 top left, flying in 1947 after 602 Squadron was formed.

Restored to flying condition by July 1950, LA198 was stored at 33 MU Lyneham until issued to No. 3 Civilian Anti-Aircraft Co-operation Unit at Exeter on 19 September 1951. Now in an overall silver finish, it carried the single code letter B and flew with this unit until 19 November 1953, when it was retired to 9 MU Cosford as non-effective stock. On 19 February 1954, it was allocated the maintenance serial 7118M and issued to No. 187 (City of Worcester) Squadron, Air Training Corps, as an instructional airframe. It remained with the ATC at Worcester until January 1967. In 1967 it was loaned to Spitfire Productions Ltd for use in the film *The Battle of Britain*, where it was seen masquerading as N3316. During this time, various parts were removed as spares for airworthy machines, but by August 1968 it was physically complete and placed in storage at 71 MU Henlow, Bedfordshire. The following year it was allocated to RAF Locking near Bristol for display purposes where it was restored to its original markings of No.1(F) Squadron and mounted on a plinth at the station gate.

From the early 1980s there had been a continuous effort to have the Spitfire brought north for display at Glasgow Airport. Approaches to the Royal Air Force through Lord Provosts of Glasgow, Members of Parliament and others were to no avail, so it was a stroke of good fortune that it came to RAF Leuchars – whose then Spitfire gate guardian was required elsewhere – in April 1986. The Station Commander of RAF Leuchars at that time, Group Capt Ian Macfadyen, was visiting the 602 Museum in Glasgow earlier that year and was made aware of LA198's strong links with Glasgow. That evening, at a dinner in the city, he said he would make it his personal responsibility to have the aircraft restored to its 602 markings and dedicated to the memory of the Squadron.

Sadly, in 1989, RAF policy dictated that all Spitfire gate guardians should be removed as the weather was rapidly deteriorating their condition. LA198 went south and was stored firstly at St Athan, Vale of Glamorgan, and then Cardington, Bedfordshire, to await a decision on its future. It was, in fact, being held for possible use as a swap for another historic aircraft. Pressure continued to have it returned to Glasgow and it was through the good offices of the then Air Officer Scotland & Northern Ireland, Air Commodore Jack Haines, in a conversation with Michael Forsyth, then Secretary of State for Scotland, that the RAF were persuaded by Michael Portillo, then UK Secretary of State for Defence, to release the Spitfire.

In November 1996 it was announced that it would be returned to Scotland and gifted to the City of Glasgow where it would be displayed as a lasting tribute to the men and women of the City's Squadron. On 4 March 1998 the aircraft was transported north, stopping outside the 602 Museum at Hillington on its way to East Fortune for restoration. Its return to the City in such splendid condition marks a happy end to its travels.

Top

This is one of the more unusual objects found when stripping LA198 – a mouse nest.

Bottom

Rusty port wing bay.

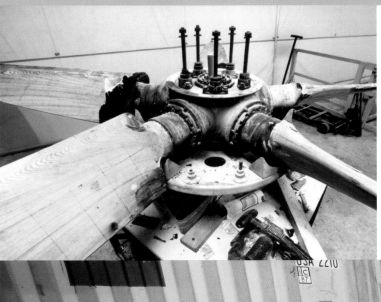

Top

LA198's five blade propeller stripped prior to restoration.

Bottom

Ray removing the covers from the fully restored propeller.

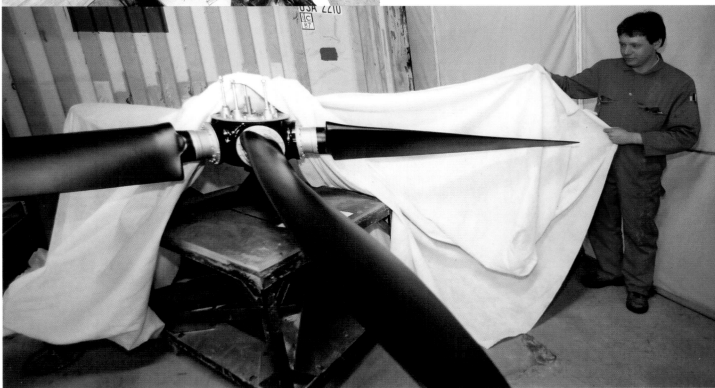

The restoration

Top

Wing stripped prior to restoration.

Bottom

Ray and Bert checking the paint finish on one of the wings.

Top

LA198's restored Rolls Royce Griffon engine with the fuselage in the background.

Bottom

Kyle working on the tail fin.

Top

Bert making some adjustments in the cockpit of LA198.

Bottom

LA198 fully restored and being moved onto display at The Museum of Flight, East Fortune.

Spitfire LA198 restored

Original details of LA198
Wingspan 36 feet 11 inches; length 32 feet 8 inches; weight normal maximum take-off 11,290lbs; max speed 450mph
at 19,000 feet; range (clean) 580 miles; serial no. (manufacturer's c/n)–13658; cockpit data plate SMAF 4338.

The formation of the Squadron

602 Squadron was the very first auxiliary squadron created by Lord Trenchard, the great early Chief of the Air Staff. He had the idea of a territory-based civilian force, a 'corps d'elite' of the air, and so it was agreed in the early 1920s that a number of squadrons would be established. They were to be based in centres of population where not only would there be a local pool of air crew, but also, which was very important, where there would be engineering expertise to maintain the aircraft. Glasgow was one of the foremost centres for engineering at that time, and 602 Squadron was fortunate in having that expertise close at hand.

On 12th September 1925 Flight Lieutenant Dan Martyn, newly appointed as the regular adjutant, arrived at Renfrew Aerodrome, where 602 Squadron was to be based. At that time the airfield was somewhat run down, having been a wartime acceptance park for aircraft built by Clydeside shipbuilding and engineering companies during the First World War. With his arrival 602 Squadron was in business, and was, by a clear month, the first Auxiliary Air Force Squadron. The City of Edinburgh, 603 Squadron, came a month later at Turnhouse, and in June 1937 the County of Aberdeen, 612 Squadron, was formed at Dyce.

The Squadron flew from Renfrew Aerodrome, first in DH9As and Avro 504Ks and then in the Fairey Fawn. After the Fawns the pilots flew Westland Wapitis, and there are some intriguing photographs of Wapitis taking off from Renfrew with Arkleston Cemetery in the background. Today travellers going between Glasgow and Glasgow International Airport (now at Abbotsinch) pass by Arkleston Cemetery exactly as it was in these early days, and in fact the M8 motorway is roughly on the alignment of the old 08 runway built during the war.

As Renfrew Aerodrome was proving too small even then and the field was suffering from drainage problems, the Squadron moved to Abbotsinch in January 1933. Hawker Harts replaced the Wapitis and in turn were replaced by Hinds. 602 was originally a light bomber squadron, and for a very short period the Hinds gave way to the Hawker Hector when, in 1938, the role of the Squadron was changed to Army Co-operation duties. This was very unpopular and the Hector was rather an unpopular aeroplane, being basically the Hart Hind series developed with a Napier Dagger engine. However, the Squadron only had them for a few months before they were re-designated as a fighter squadron.

In January 1939, 602 Squadron was supplied with the Gloster Gauntlet fighter, a beautiful, very manoeuvrable, little bi-plane. They had these for a relatively short time before, on the 8th May 1939, Clydeside reverberated to the sound of the Merlin engine in the Spitfire. 602 was the first Auxiliary Air Force Squadron to receive the Spitfire and about the eighth in the Royal Air Force as a whole to receive it, so it was quite a mark of distinction that the Auxiliaries were given the RAF's new wonder fighter.

When the Spitfires were introduced, 602 received 19 aircraft. This allowed for spares and for aircraft being out of service for maintenance. There were two flights of Spitfires, 'A' and 'B'. During the early years of the war, 'B' Flight's aircraft were named after the seven dwarfs, and pilot George Pinkerton, who was a slightly taciturn individual, got the name 'Grumpy', and pilot Sandy Johnstone, being quite a suave individual, got the name 'Bashful'. 602 Squadron learnt to fly these Spitfires at Abbotsinch and the squadron was mobilized on 24th August 1939 to go to war.

World War II

The Squadron entered the war quite early, being sent first to Grangemouth and then to Drem on the east coast to protect the North Sea areas. On the 16th October 1939, 602 Squadron was in action along with 603 (City of Edinburgh) Squadron, and there has always been some debate as to which Squadron shot the first German aircraft down over Great Britain. Both of the Scottish Auxiliary Fighter Squadrons were in action, with Flight Lieutenant George Pinkerton, Flying Officer Archie McKellar and Flying Officer Paul Webb of the 602

'A' flight, 602 Squadron with George Pinkerton sitting on the propeller.

successfully shooting down a Junkers 88 (JU88) in the early afternoon, just off Crail in Fife. (603 had also just shot down a JU88 over the Forth.) The JU88s were the new wonder bombers from German Squadron KG30, flying from Westerland on Sylt.

The Squadron saw other action that day. In the morning George Pinkerton had had a go at a Heinkel from German Squadron KG26, which was probably on a reconnaissance mission. Pinkerton's adversary at that particular time was Hauptman Pohle, the commander of KG30. Coincidentally, both men were farmers, and it was hoped to have them meet again in Scotland a few years ago. Sadly, George Pinkerton died before this could be arranged.

602's finest moment – the Battle of Britain
602's finest moment could be said to be their performance during the Battle of Britain, under the leadership of Sandy Johnstone, later Air Vice-Marshal Johnstone. The Squadron came down from Drem in early August 1940 and was based at a satellite of Tangmere, Westhampnett. They performed splendidly and shot many German aircraft down during the battle. Sadly, one of their most successful former pilots, Archie McKellar, was shot down just a few hours after the Battle of Britain had been 'administratively' finished and does not feature in the Roll of Honour – he was then commanding 605 Squadron.

The Clydebank Blitz
After the Battle of Britain, 602 Squadron returned to Prestwick and was there during the Clydebank Blitz.

Fighter Command had introduced the idea of the 'fighter night', where squadrons patrolled at various height levels. Unfortunately the Luftwaffe was not co-operative and decided to come in at a level between those covered by the British aircraft, rendering the plan ineffective and causing great destruction. At the time radar was not available, and so it was very much a case of see and be seen, or be shot down using the 'mark one eyeball' (using one's eyesight).

602 went on to fight over the Channel and after D-Day was based in airfields in France and Belgium before coming back to Norfolk to disband.

The end of the Auxiliary Air Force
During the war, 602 had been encompassed into the Royal Air Force. They were reformed as an auxiliary squadron at Abbotsinch in 1946, flying Spitfire Mark 14s, 21s, and then Mark 22s. For a period they returned to Renfrew while new runways were laid at Abbotsinch. In 1954 the Squadron moved back to Abbotsinch with Vampires and Meteor trainers, but sadly the whole of the Auxiliary Air Force was disbanded in March 1957 on financial grounds. It was also suggested that the new fast jet aircraft that were being developed were not suitable for the auxiliaries, but eloquent witness to the contrary is borne by the auxiliaries in the United States, whose Reserve and National Guard fly and maintain the most advanced fighters from municipal airports.

The Naval Volunteer Reserve Squadrons, the Scottish Air Division, 1830 and 1843 Squadrons, and the Air Observation Post Squadrons of the Auxiliary Air Force, including 666 Squadron, which were really army units, also disbanded on the 10th March 1957. The Auxiliary Air Force, by then the Royal Auxiliary Air Force, still exists in a number of units, including No.2 Maritime Headquarters Unit in Edinburgh, rebadged in 1999 as 603 Squadron.

602 Squadron's pilots

There were many distinguished 602 pilots. Amongst the first members of 602 Squadron was David McIntyre, the great founder of Scottish aviation, who, together with the Marquis of Douglas and Clydesdale, later the 14th Duke of Hamilton, were the first men to fly over Everest, in Westland bi-planes in 1933. David McIntyre, who had a shipping background, had a vision for an aviation industry in Scotland, which he saw would take over from shipbuilding. Sadly, smaller and lesser men conspired to frustrate his vision, but even so we can see it still today at Prestwick and at BAE SYSTEMS, where up until a few years ago aircraft for the world were designed and built. Other distinguished pilots included Hector MacLean, Findlay Boyd, Glen Niven, Donald Jack, J. Dunlop Urie, Marcus Robinson, Sandy Johnstone (who commanded the Squadron in the Battle of Britain), and George Pinkerton. All went on to distinguish themselves in the Air Force as a whole, gaining high rank. Hector MacLean, who had been one of the early 1930s' pilots in 602 and who had had his foot blown off and his leg badly damaged in the Battle of Britain, came back to command 3602 Squadron, the Fighter Control Unit at Bishopbriggs, but by that time radar had been developed and Fighter Control Units really had become obsolete. 2602 Squadron, also at Bishopbriggs, was the light anti-aircraft Airfield Defence Squadron.

Also flying with 602 were people who become well known in the media, like Raymond Baxter. 'Bax' flew with 602 towards the end of the war on some raids on the Low Countries, particularly on the Shell Mex building in The Hague. He talks interestingly of the raid led by another very vigorous character, Max Sutherland, who commanded the Squadron at that time. One of the many allied airmen who served with 602 was Pierre Closterman of the Free French, who wrote a number of books, including *The Big Show*, of his time in the Royal Air Force.

One of the apocryphal stories attached to the Squadron involves the pilot J. Dunlop Urie who took up a brand new Spitfire on an operational patrol, and within about 10 minutes was shot up. He forced landed the aircraft, but it was written off, probably the shortest operational life of a Spitfire! There are photographs of it with the bullet holes in it, and it has been said that his father, who ran City Bakeries, bought another one!

602 Museum

On 28th October 1939, a Heinkel 111 was shot down near Humbie, East Lothian, by the combined efforts of 602 and 603 Squadrons, the first enemy aircraft to fall on British soil. Rolls Royce sent a team to examine the engines and one of their engineers, Willie Gilmartin, 'acquired' a couple of panels from the aircraft. In 1982, Willie, who had been a civilian instructor with the 2175 (Rolls Royce) Squadron Air Training Corps at Hillington, presented the panels to its then commanding officer, Flt Lt Bill McConnell. From what began as a kind of research project for the cadets, a museum was built in the ATC compound by the cadets under the leadership of Bill McConnell. The cadets had discovered that there was no other commemoration of the city's illustrious Fighter Squadron and determined to do something about it. Material and memorabilia were, and have since been, donated and lent, and an association formed.

The museum was opened on the 22nd October 1983 by the Marshal of the Royal Air Force, Lord Cameron of Balhousie, a fitting memorial to 602 (City of Glasgow) Squadron Royal Auxiliary Air Force and all who served in it from 1925 to 1957.

To end on a personal note, to me this aircraft means recollections of my boyhood when I lived in Yoker. One Sunday morning I went over with my father on our bikes to Renfrew, and I remember seeing the Spitfires. This must have been the summer of 1950, and these Spitfires were very different Spitfires from the ones that were in the Spitfire books. They had bubble canopies and had big fins and were the Mark 22s, but the Mark 21s and the 22s flew together right up until the end. I remember being inspired and seeing the pilots with their leather helmets and their oxygen masks, and desperately wanting to do that – that's what I wanted to be, a fighter pilot and nothing else. I didn't quite make that, although I did learn to fly at Abbotsinch and flew light aircraft there from the West of Scotland Flying Club.

Dugald Cameron

F/O Raymond Baxter (second from left) briefing 602 pilots for the raid on the Shell Mex building, The Hague, 17th March 1945.

'Coming Home' by Dugald Cameron, showing Spitfire LA198 with FR.X1Ve, TP236, over Abbotsinch in 1947.

These are the transcripts of some of the oral histories taken from pilots of 602 (City of Glasgow) Squadron, commissioned by Glasgow Museums from the Digital Design Studio at Glasgow School of Art. The histories are reproduced as the men remembered and told them, and any additions we have made to the text are indicated in square brackets.

During the war certain words, which are asterisked in the following histories, were in common use to describe the enemy armed forces. Usage should be seen in the context of the pilots' experiences and of the time, and does not imply acceptance of the terms by Glasgow City Council.

Alex Robertson
Curator, Social History and Transport
Museum of Transport, Glasgow

Well, I thought flying was the thing of the future and I wanted to be able to fly. I also didn't approve of Hitler and reckoned we were going to be at war with him. So, I thought I'd combine the two by joining the (Royal) Auxiliary Air Force.

That was first of all, before I started my university degree, and then I was interviewed by Lord Clydesdale. When I realized the amount of work required for the Auxiliary Air Force and the amount of time, I realized I would never get my degree. So I had to put it off until I graduated in 1935, and I went back to Renfrew, to Abbotsinch, and was accepted into the Auxiliary Air Force.

The first aircraft that I flew was an Avro 504N. It was a dual-training aeroplane. Curiously enough it was the same aeroplane that my uncle, as Commandant of the Central Flying School in 1916, had trained his pilots on, which shows you how much money the RAF spent on their trainers. It cruised at 75mph. Very cold. I loved it. Went up with D F McIntyre who was a famous pilot in the West of Scotland, he was my first instructor. He was very good too.

My first encounter in a Spitfire was in May 1939. We were the first auxiliary squadron to get them. I think they chose us because Abbotsinch was very big, much bigger than most aerodromes, and it was reckoned that we needed a lot of room to make sure they got down. So we were lucky, we got them early in 1939 but there was nothing we could train on. So we had to eventually take a three-hour examination, on paper, on how to fly them and we all sat this examination and passed, but it wasn't quite the same as flying it. We had to study the manuals, you see, and all about the different knobs or what they call, or used to call, the tits, and we had to be watched. That was while we were all doing our jobs in Glasgow, we would study in our spare time, you see. So anyway, we passed and went on to do our first solos – that was the moment of truth.

The Spitfire had two positions on the prop. One normal and one fine pitch for take off. And you took off in fine pitch and as I opened my throttle and got underway I began to wonder if I was in the right pitch. I pulled the lever and it went into coarse and then I realized I wasn't going to get off so I went back into fine. And then I started pumping up the wheels. I got off the ground, managed to get over the high tension wires over the Cart and then when the wheels were up it simply sailed away. I was over Bearsden before I hardly knew where I was. It was a wonderful experience. When I got down the adjutant was very cross. He threatened to put me off flying and that was it. Anyway, I think he was told to shut up by the CO (Commanding Officer) so I went on.

It was a lovely aeroplane to fly but it had terrible problems for the beginner. If you weren't frightfully careful you'd go on your nose, particularly if there was any mud. Because, you see, there was such a huge engine forward of the wheels so the centre of gravity was really too far forward. The slightest interruption; if

your wheels stuck in the ground you could go on the nose and break your prop. That's where we had most of our accidents. I'm glad to say that didn't happen to me.

Of course another trouble was the flame exuded from the side of the engines, through the kidney tubes, made landing at night extremely hazardous. Another little problem was the fact that you had to pump up the wheels by a large black lever on the right hand side of the cockpit. And that meant that you took your hand off the throttle and put it onto the control column. And you were flying the thing off, after take off you were flying it with the wrong hand and if you'd forgotten to tighten your throttle quadrant you could be in trouble.

We were not prepared for night flying when the war broke out, but for day flying, yes. We were quite confident. Probably more confident than we really ought to have been, but it was no bad thing that.

The squadron started at Abbotsinch, we mobilized there. We moved to Grangemouth about a fortnight or a month later than that for a few days. And then Douglas Farquhar, our CO, was told to investigate whether Drem in East Lothian was a suitable place for the squadron. It was the obvious place for the defence of Glasgow on the east coast. So I was sent off to have breakfast at Drem and to see if it was fit to land on. It had a kind of a grassy wet strip right across the aerodrome at the bottom of it and I was warned not to go on my nose. Well, I managed to get down without going on my nose, had breakfast and came back. The squadron moved off next morning to Drem. I never quite understood whether Douglas thought I was a safe pair of hands or whether it was if MacLean can do it anybody can!

So then after Drem we went to Montrose and back to Drem and then down south to a place called Westhampnett for the Battle of Britain. During the Battle of the Forth, which was fought from Drem and Turnhouse, I attacked a couple of 88s without any great results, I don't think. I wasted time because I was looking for swastikas on the enemy and I couldn't believe that they really were enemy until I got close enough to see if they were and then I saw they had black crosses. So then I knew they really must be the enemy. By that time I'd lost a lot of time, I fired off all my bullets, but whether those aircraft got back or not I don't know. The real trouble was that Fighter Command had decreed a bullet grouping that, instead of concentrating the fire at one point in front of the fighter, was spread along the wings of an imaginary target. Also we were told to open fire at 400 yards, which was far too distant. And the result was that both 602 and 603 expended about 18,000 rounds of ammunition. I think about four of the Huns* didn't get back to Germany. Two came down of course in Scotland.

The Battle of Britain was going on in July and the Huns* were attacking shipping in the Channel but that phase was nearly over. We were sent down to relieve 145 Squadron at Westhampnett [Sussex], I think they only had about four pilots left and so we came in to relieve them on the 13th of August. We were on duty from then on. On the 16th, I think it was, we had an attack on a naval aerodrome on the coast, a place called Ford. Now this I think was a mistake, I think the Huns* thought it was a fighter field. Anyway, they sent a huge formation of dive-bombers, JU87s. So we got in amongst that lot, but the 109s got on our tails and my flight commander Dunlop Urie was very badly shot up. When he got back to Westhampnett there were huge holes all through his aeroplane but he managed to land, and they whisked him off to hospital. And I became Flight Commander of 'A' Flight and so I went on until the 26th when I stopped a cannon shell. I managed to get the aeroplane back to Westhampnett without my right foot, which was dangling down in my shoe. So I was carted off to hospital. So that was the end of my operational flying career. Later in the war I got my medical category back but it was towards the end of the war and I reckoned that if I went on into bombers I wouldn't be properly trained until it was finished. So I thought I'd better just stay on the staff. So I didn't volunteer for any more ops.

I took the, what they call, the controllers course, down in Woodlands at Stanmore. And this trained us to be what they call sector controllers. That is, we were able to tell the fighters, from in the control room, that the fighters and the bombers were plotted. It was our job to vector the fighters into the path of bombers so that they intercepted. And for that you had to be rather specially trained so there was a special course for that. And it was rather amusing; the course had a practical side to it. They converted a whole lot of ice cream tricycles and put radio into them and these tricycles would simulate a piece of territory on the lawn of Woodlands at Clamphill. An intriguing business, it would appeal to caricaturists.

I returned northwards as a controller in time for the Clydeside Blitz. I was on duty at Rosemount House near Monkton, that was where the West of Scotland were controlling the defences, from Rosemount. These bombers were seen approaching, I think both up the Irish Sea and across the North Sea, I can't remember. But anyway, the command, the group at Newcastle, ordered what is called a fighter night. So we threw up all the night fighters we had. We had things called Defiants at that point, they weren't much good but they

Above: Relaxing between missions in the crew room at Drem, March 1940. Left to right: Donald Jack, P.J.Strong, Archie McKellar (lying down), Cyril Babbage and Hector MacLean.

were the only thing we had for night. So we sent all the Defiants up we could. I think they only got one actually, but it was a rather exasperating evening or night because I knew I couldn't win.

The night watch was on and the Defiants were responsible for the defence. By that time they'd realized the Spitfire was a useless thing at night, or very nearly useless. However, when news got round at the base I think Sandy Johnstone went off in a Spitfire and I don't know if anybody else did, to see what he could find. But he didn't find anything. But the rest of the chaps were stood down for the night, had gone home, obviously. Gone back to their quarters no doubt, but they were a day fighter squadron.

There was another raid the following night; I think there were two raids. I wasn't on the second one. I got the Sector Commander up, a man called Loel Guinness and the Senior Controller, they came up but they couldn't do any more than I could.

Funnily enough, about a month later I was on a short leave at Kilmacolm here and I went down to look at Greenock. It was an absolute shambles. I'd never thought that Greenock would recover at all by the look of it. And you wouldn't know now.

At night you can't see the enemy unless the searchlights pick it up. I don't know how many searchlights they had at Clydebank and Greenock but they only got one that way. And the anti-aircraft got, I think they claimed one at a slightly lower altitude. Night

fighting without a real good cluster of searchlights intercepting on the targets is rather like just swatting a fly in a darkened out room. That is, until we got the radar, I was involved in that, but that came later.

We were very well prepared for the war considering the Germans had no radar protection at all and knew nothing about it. We had a system evolved by 'Stuffy' Dowding of radar stations all round the coast. We would have been defeated in the Battle of Britain without that. The night side we hadn't developed, we hadn't been able to find the answer. We only got it in about 1941/42 in the form of a thing called a GCI. That was where you could actually look into the screen and see the aeroplanes flying across a map, about a foot in diameter, in a blacked out van. And this GCI enabled you to get the fighter in behind the bomber. And then the fighters, night fighters, were also equipped with radar. If we, on the ground, could get the fighter close enough, the radar operator would tell the radar operator in the aeroplane to flash his weapon. And he would flash it, put it on. And, lo and behold, he would be able to see the image of the bomber ahead and the pilot would close in on it and destroy it, which was quite a lengthy operation. We would only do it one at a time.

On the 10th of May 1941, I was on the watch at Rosemount, and we'd had no hostile aircraft on the table at all since the control room opened. Suddenly there was a hostile plotted somewhere near Selkirk, heading west, and I had two Defiants up and they were practising their AI; they'd just received their air interception radar equipment and were practising it. So as they were fully armed I told them to orbit Kilmarnock, and, of course the Southern Uplands had got very very few Observer Corps, so I phoned up the Observer Corps man and said 'You've got a hostile there, what is it?'. He said 'It's a Messerschmitt 110'. I said 'For goodness sake, it hasn't got enough petrol to get back to Germany. I think you'd better tell your chaps to have another look'. So I warned our Defiants that it might just be a friendly so anyway, they never found the 110, and about an hour later, I suppose about 11 o'clock, the phone went.

This was a sergeant at the police station at Eaglesham, I think it was, and he said there was a German captain had bailed out of his aeroplane and was in custody at the police station. And he said he wanted to speak to the Duke of Hamilton. I said 'Well, what does he want?'. 'He won't say anything, he wants to speak to the Duke of Hamilton so, I knew where the Duke was, he was the Section Commander on the east side, the Section Commander of the whole of the defences on the east side of Scotland at Turnhouse. So I got through to the controller at Turnhouse on the phone, but the Duke had gone for the night. So I said 'You'll have to get him, I must speak to him'. There was a bit of a kind of delay and I got put through to his house from the station. A man answered the phone and was very cautious; he didn't want to say what had happened to the Duke, where the Duke was. And I said 'Has he gone to bed?' 'Well yes'. So we had to get him up. The Duke came on the line, a very tetchy voice. 'What's all this Hector?' I said 'Well there's this German

captain in Eaglesham police station wants to talk to you'. He said 'What does he want to speak to me about?'. I said 'Well he won't say'. Then there was a bit of a pause, doubtless thinking it out. 'What do you think I should do about this?' Just gaining time, if you want my opinion really. But anyway, I said 'I think you'd better go and ask him yourself' and so he said 'Yes I think I will'. And so it was left like that, and the rest of the story is public knowledge.

The rumour went around very fast that it was Rudolph Hess. In fact, I think the army who were looking after him had more or less twigged who he was, or who he was supposed to be. My part in it was very small. But the interesting fact was, I only discovered many years after the war that Hess told them that he'd seen my Defiants, thought they were Hurricanes, decided his number was up and bailed out. So in a sense, I was responsible, possibly, for saving his life because if he'd tried to land at Hamilton's Emergency Field at Dungavel in a 110 he would have killed himself. So perhaps I saved the poor chap's life.

I was put in charge of training controllers at Prestwick. And then, all the raids would come in more or less from the eastside but the Huns* came up the Irish Sea and instead of coming to us they turned left and gave Belfast a pasting. And the Northern Irish government didn't like it. So there was a tremendous build up of the defence, ground defences against air attack in Northern Ireland. And I was sent across to be the Staff Officer in charge of it. So I went over there in 1942 and once there I couldn't get out. Nobody would come to replace me. However, I went on… but there weren't very many raids in Northern Ireland, hardly any. So I was once again put in charge of training controllers. But after I think about a year on the staff I was made Senior Controller of Northern Ireland. Then I was finally posted down to Senior Controller as one of the duty controllers in charge of the defence of London. That was in early 1944. And then I was Senior Controller at a place called Middle Wallop in the West of England.

By this time the end of the war was a foregone conclusion. The flying bombs were coming in, of course, when I was controlling the defences over London. But there was not much we could do about them. And the rockets, of course, you could just do nothing about them at all. Then of course after that our ground forces were getting across into Germany by this time or were across the Rhine. So, after that it was a question of trying to keep the spirits or the optimism up, because there wasn't enough to do for the troops, it was quite a problem. But we tried to cope with that. And we had to keep the British control system going because if the invasion had come to grief, or the Russians had failed they could turn their attention back on to us again. And, of course, we still had the Japs* to deal with and that meant a tremendous demand for more and more controllers and ground staff. So we were training them for that. But we didn't know that the atomic bomb was coming.

I finished the war at, what they call, Wing Commander Plans at Drumossie, Inverness. Which was just a matter of laying on exercises for the fighters to keep them in trim really, that's what it was for. Fortunately I had enough experience down at 11 Group and the staff to be able to do that until I was released. I flew more as a staff officer to visit all the GCI stations and fighter stations that we had under our control. I used to go and see the squadrons and so on and talk to them about problems and all that sort of thing. Of course it was one of the pleasanter sides of the staff work to do that, we enjoyed it.

Oh, the war was something I wouldn't have missed. A great experience. But of course it didn't do my profession, working as a solicitor, any good, because I came back to work as a solicitor six years after graduating and I had to get down to it. It's extraordinary how much one can remember after so many years.

A very interesting thing happened on one occasion. I went to the dentist just after the war, and I said 'I've never had gas', to take this tooth out you see, I said 'I think I might like to try gas to see what it's like'. And I got gassed and I came to and my tooth was gone, but the poor old dentist was sweating with exhaustion. And apparently, as soon as I went under I started flying an aeroplane in a battle!

Well, I was at Glasgow Academy and left school and we had a family business. A very unlikely business, making children's clothes. So it doesn't sound very much like a Spitfire pilot but I hated the job. I trained as a salesman, which did enable me to get about quite a lot.

I mean, by the mid 1930s it was obvious that Hitler was up to no good; there'd be no holding him back unless there was some resistance. And a lot of young fellows at that time started thinking about what they would do. Well, army life had never appealed to me very much, I'd once gone to annual camp with the Glasgow Academy OTC [Officers Training Corps] and I realized then that army life was not for me. And a brother of a great friend of mine was in 602 Squadron and we were invited to a garden party at what was known then as 'Empire Air Day', when various squadrons in various stations were open to the public, and flying displays and that sort of thing. And it was then, that was in 1935, that I got my first taste of what flying would be like and it appealed to me from the word go, I thought 'This is for me'. We certainly didn't join with our eyes shut; we didn't just join for the flying.

So, eventually, when I joined 602 in 1936, and started flying in 1937, I'd plenty of time as a salesman travelling about you see. So I could spend quite a lot of time at Abbotsinch and it was a very demanding business flying in 602 because we flew three weekends a month and in the summer, two evenings a week. So it didn't leave you a great deal of spare time. One weekend a month we generally got together and played golf or sailed or skied, depending on what time of the year. So my life was very much taken up by 602 and flying. I think to indulge in that sort of life you've got to be really dedicated to flying, we all loved it and there was a big bond between us.

I started flying in Moths, which were lovely little aeroplanes and I had to join the Scottish Flying Club at Renfrew to get this training. Normally you were trained from the word go by the Adjutant or the Assistant Adjutant of the squadron, but they had no Assistant Adjutant when I joined, so I went over at His Majesty's expense and got an 'A' licence [the original private pilot's licence] at the flying club, these gorgeous little Moths, really super. When I came back into 602 for further training I was relegated to a thing called an Avro 504N, which was an adaptation without the skid from an old First War type. It was good for learning, it was good for aerobatics and it went flat out at about 80 mph. So, that was the thing and then the first real aircraft I flew was a Hawker Hart because at that time the 602 was a light bomber squadron, so I flew for some months in a Hawker Hart. Then graduated upwards to a Hawker Hind, as the squadron was re-equipped, again, a light bomber, and I went through all the bomb training syllabus. But, eventually, it was decided by the powers that be that the bombing syllabus was far too complicated for weekend flyers. So we were transferred to Army Co-operation and issued with an aircraft not

unlike a Hawker Hart or Hind, called a Hawker Hector. But instead of being powered by a Rolls Royce Merlin engine it was powered with a Napier Dagger, which was a huge great H section engine and made this aircraft the worst I have flown in my life, it was horrible. But luckily they didn't keep us in Army Co-operation for very long and we switched again to Fighter Command, who were equipped with Gloster Gauntlets. That was a very nice aeroplane, light as a feather, very manoeuvrable, very aerobatic. We started being equipped with Spitfires in May '39. And I flew my first Spitfire on 4th of June 1939 and it was terrific, absolutely wonderful.

Then 602 Squadron was mobilized on the 24th of August '39. And we then became professionals overnight. We lived really in limbo at Abbotsinch until about the beginning of October when we were moved forward to RAF Station Drem in East Lothian. Our role at that time was really giving cover to defensive east coast convoys. And we spent hours and hours, sometimes in filthy weather, covering these convoys as they slowly steamed up the east coast to Methil Bay, on the Firth of Forth.

On the 16th of October we were suddenly in action for the first time as the Luftwaffe sent over 18 JU88s to attack either the Forth Railway Bridge or riverside [it was in fact to attack shipping, as they believed that HMS *Hood* would be there], we were never quite sure which. But they were intercepted by two auxiliary squadrons, our own 602, and 603, the Edinburgh auxiliary squadron. Two aircraft, two of the Germans, were shot down and others were damaged. I wasn't particularly successful, I wasn't able to claim anything, but I think I hit one of them on his way out. But, the flight I was with had Dunlop Urie as the leader and the excitement when they got back to Drem was terrific. Before that, I must say, as I turned away from my enemy another JU88 passed right in front of my sights but I had no ammunition left so there was nothing I could do about it, but it was really galling because he was just there. However, when we got back there was terrific excitement, the reaction at that time was odd because, you must understand, we had never fired our guns in anger before. The reaction was, 'Had I killed someone? Did that aircraft which was limping along very badly when we left it, did it get back or did it go down in the sea?'. But anyway, we had a terrific celebration that night in Edinburgh Caledonian Hotel, and then we got back to our normal duties together and we just kept on doing these wretched convoy patrols and night patrols too, which were murder in a Spitfire.

Even just getting out onto the airfield you would have an airman on each wing tip because a Spitfire was very blind on the ground – it had this huge nose that stuck up in the air. So you had really to move your nose backwards and forwards so that you could see where you were going. But at night we were just flying off with a flare path of paraffin lamps. It was pretty fraught because you'd probably been taxiing on the ground for quite a few minutes and the engine had got very hot and when you opened up to full throttle the glare from

the exhaust stubs was blinding. So it was very difficult just to keep your line on the flare path to see if you were going in the right direction. Then when you eventually took off you had to forget about the flare path, get your head inside the cockpit and onto your instruments. Now that was fine, but it was difficult seeing the instruments sometimes because you were still dazzled by the flare off of the exhaust. But not only that, the instruments, the rate of climb instrument and your artificial horizon, when you first lifted off, appeared to read that you were diving and that you were losing height. This would go on for maybe eight or ten seconds so you just had to remember that you were not losing height, and then the instruments would settle down and off you'd go. But it was very fraught, landing was not much fun either. So 602 were the only squadron at Drem who were night operational. And all the others in the Turnhouse sector never forgave our CO, for saying that we were night operational.

That went on till about the end of '39 and that meant the few of us who were experienced were on duty, night duty, at least twice a week. That was pretty tasking, you had to sleep in the hut. I may confess for my own part, that when I was up at night, and you must bear in mind that this was total black out and sometimes the weather wasn't all that good, my main preoccupation was to get myself safely down on the ground again. Because to pick out an enemy aircraft in the air at night was nearly impossible, and I firmly believe that it was only done so that some politician in the House of Parliament could say that when the enemy attacks, our fighters went up and drove them off.

However, we did achieve one success at night when Sandy Johnstone, our new C.O., shot down a Dornier. I think it was very near Dunbar. And it was the first enemy aircraft we shot down on land. That was a beautiful June night and it couldn't be more perfect for night flying. After that went on we were waiting at the end of April and May to be moved south to cover the Dunkirk evacuation. It never came our way, we waited, we were all ready, packed up, ready to go down at a moment's notice. So we had to bide our time. On the 13th of August we were posted off to Tangmere section, for the Battle of Britain. When we arrived there was an almighty dogfight going on up above us. The squadron that we were going to relieve was 145 Squadron. We went into the mess for the first time, and Paul Webb who you may have heard of, he was another

member of 602, was in the mess before us, he said, 'Meet 145 Squadron, all three of them'. So that wasn't a very good sort of welcoming talk. However, we got quickly down to work, Sandy Johnstone was a magnificent leader, and we had various encounters at any height from 15,000 to about 25,000 feet.

The number of aircraft steadily increased as we got on towards the middle of September when Hitler had decided that he should invade or he would be too late. Now I'm convinced that he had every intention of invading but he reckoned that he had to have air superiority before he could risk it, and by the grace of God, he never got that. So there have been many accounts told of various incidents and individual battles and so on. But my most vivid recollection of it was on

'Glasgow's Own'. The Lord Provost of Glasgow Patrick (Paddy) Dolan with 602 Squadron outside the City Chambers in 1940. The Duke of Hamilton and Sandy Johnstone are standing side by side, third and second from the right in the back row.

the 7th of September over Kent. We intercepted a vast number of German bombers all escorted by fighters buzzing round them. It reminded me very much of geese on migration, flight after flight as far back as you could see, aircraft upon aircraft, squadron after squadron. A little voice on the R.T. said it all for us, it said, 'Jesus Christ! It's the whole ruddy Luftwaffe!' and that's what it looked like. However it was quite a difficult problem attacking this vast number, how to go about it, because we'd never seen so many before. But we did see Archie McKellar lead his squadron of Hurricanes, he had already been promoted and was a squadron commander. And he did a head on attack and it was wonderful. It came right through the first flight of German bombers and the whole line just wobbled and disintegrated and the whole mass of course just kept on coming, but it was a wonderful attack. We had to attack from the side because that's where we were positioned when we saw them. And I made no claim; I don't think I shot anything down but I saw lots of pieces coming off. The difficulty was getting away from it because the tendency would be to dive away but you get a hail of bullets from all the low rear gunners. So however, I got back to Tangmere very happily.

It was all in the melting pot then. All we wanted to do was to win this battle because we knew that the Germans' intention was to invade. And very early on, towards the end of August, we came to a thing called 'Red Alert' which meant that invasion was imminent within hours. So all we were thinking about at that time was preventing this invasion. We didn't really think any further ahead than that, in fact we lived day by day.

People said there was a lot of bravery, I always questioned that because we had to do it, it was orders. And if we hadn't done we would have had an awful fate. There were a few cases of a lack of moral fibre, in other words poor fellows losing their nerve, so what we were interested in was surviving the day and ready for the next day, generally with a dram or two at night to steady us up. No drugs, no drugs at all, and no counselling, we just had to get the hell on with it ourselves.

We didn't consider ourselves as 'the few', not at that time. I think in my memoirs I say, what is now called the Battle of Britain, it wasn't that in our time. It may have been the banner headlines in *The Mirror* and that sort of thing but we didn't recognize it as the Battle of Britain, at least I didn't anyway.

We got a tremendous lot of publicity in Glasgow, in the papers. The Lord Provost of Glasgow at that time, Sir Paddy Dolan, was a great fan of 602 Squadron and he saw that we got a lot of publicity. None of it we particularly wanted, but it did bring us in a lot of money that eventually became 602's Benevolent Fund. And with that we were able to have money available after the war for fellows who really needed a bit of financial help. So that was one good thing the publicity did. I think Glasgow was interested in what we were doing because it was mainly Glasgow men who were featuring in the battle and in the squadron. I mentioned earlier Archie McKellar, he was one of our star turns in 602. Another Glasgow man, Finlay Boyd, both of them were DSO [Distinguished Service Order], DFC [Distinguished Flying Cross] and bar early on in the war, so they were really hot stuff. The end of the operation that became known as the Battle of Britain was declared over at the end of October 1939, and we had obviously diverted Hitler from his plans. Yes, I think that from October until the end of the year, when I left the 602, there was a decidedly lighter atmosphere about. The nights got longer and the flying days got shorter so we entertained ourselves more and more. But I will say this, once the battle was declared over, the actual daytime flying became more difficult and terribly frustrating because our aircraft could start tailing off, our Mark 1 Spitfires could start tailing off in power at about 27– 28,000 feet. Now the Germans with their 109s were always above us, they could still operate at about 35,000 feet. So they were always above us and it was very difficult for us, always being below them. The trick was to try and get them down to your level, but they weren't always tempted to come down, so we were very vulnerable. So you had to keep your eyes open and your wits about you, otherwise you would be bounced. And at that height you weren't terribly manoeuvrable, so I'll say it was equally hazardous at that stage as it was during the actual battle itself but for a different reason in that we were outgunned – well, not outgunned – but outmanoeuvred by the enemy.

We fought every day almost, German 109s and 110s. But the encounters were not like the First World War where there were real dogfights and everyone doing aerobatics left, right, and centre. Our whole tactic was a series of tight turns at full throttle, hoping that you could turn inside your opponent if you could do a

tighter turn than he could. And that he couldn't get on your tail, the object was to get on each other's tail and shoot. The great trick was to get your turn as tight as possible and at full throttle and you could, the really clever boys could, get speed down to about 80mph in a tight turn at full throttle. But I could never get it down much below 90, I hadn't the, I don't know what, to do it. It worked all right though. The encounters were very brief, and it would be all over in seconds, or it felt like seconds. And the next minute the air would be totally devoid of aircraft, everything was moving at such speed.

I was shot up, never shot down. Hit, yes, that was a salutary feeling. It was like being, the aircraft being... hit with a sledgehammer. Particularly if it was one of the cannon shells from the 109 it was pretty horrible. But by that time we had got armoured plating and pilots were protected to a fair degree by this armoured plating down the back of your seat, the back of your head. The only thing was that for some reason or other the armour plating left your feet and ankles exposed to shrapnel and we had quite a number of fellows who got shrapnel in their feet and legs. In fact Hector MacLean had his foot shot off, which wasn't very nice for him. But, luckily, I was never shot down.

The Spitfire was totally marvellous. If you bear in mind that I never flew any of the heavy aircraft like Lancasters and Hampdens and Wellingtons, naturally. My experience was all in medium and light aircraft. And the Spitfire, tiny little all-metal single seat, had the most amazing performance and wonderful handling characteristics; it was really beautiful to fly. And remarkably easy too, in daylight. I always remember my first flight in June '39 and really, on opening the throttle I was off the ground and in a steep climb before I really knew what was happening. And it was terrific, absolutely wonderful, the power of this Merlin engine; over a thousand horse power compared to the earlier Kestrels that we'd flown had about 500 or 600 horse power, but this was marvellous. And with its low wing and its perfect streamlining it was a wonderful fast aeroplane. It's easy to fly, I got back to Abbotsinch, landed, having been told over and over again what to do and to be word perfect on all the drills. Coming in and landing, it just landed as easily as could be. It almost landed itself. Its manoeuvrability I think was one of the great features.

When you start a Spitfire in preparation for take off in daylight you would do the minimum of taxiing because we had to be off the ground within three minutes of the order coming through to take off, or scramble as it was called in those days. So very often in the Battle of Britain when you were flying as a squadron we would be lined out on the lower side of the airfield, rush out to our aircraft, get in, strap in, and wait for the leader to give the sign to start. And off you'd all go and it was a wonderful thing. It must have been a bit like singing in some huge chorus, a Verdi chorus, because you'd have all these engines, 12 engines, roaring away beside you in fairly close formation. I always remember the first time I led the squadron off, what a marvellous feeling of exhilaration it was to look out both sides, see all these aircraft waiting for you to give the signal and away you would go. But, when you were flying at Drem

and just doing individual patrols with perhaps two or three aircraft in patrol, you might have to taxi quite a long way. Being blind, the aircraft having this huge flat nose in front of you, you had to manoeuvre, swing the nose round left to right as you taxied along to make sure you didn't go into a ditch or a hole in the ground or something. But once you were in position down wind, it was a lovely thing. You didn't bother, you didn't have flaps, you had to be what was known as fine pitch, which was the equivalent of a low gear in a motorcar. Open the throttle and away you would go. Get your wheels up almost as soon as possible, almost as soon as you got your aircraft off the ground, get the wheels up, they were retractable, it just meant moving a lever down at your right hand, and away you would go. It was all very easy. I imagine flying today with the G-suits and this, that, and the other thing it must be a very different proposition, taking off in a Tornado or Harrier or something like that.

Spitfires were pretty viceless. The Mark 1, the original Spitfire, the Mark 5 – a lovely aeroplane, a little more powerful than the 1, and then the Mark 9 which was the most glorious Spitfire to fly. Rolls Royce had developed the Merlin engine to give a great deal more power than originally. So they were faultless. Then they began tinkering with them and putting in a bigger engine, they put in a Rolls Royce Griffon engine which was about 2500 horsepower, and of course it weighed a lot more. It spoiled the centre of gravity and stability of the aircraft, and then they cut the wing tips off which gave you less lift. By that time you became kind of wary as to what you did, even a straightforward loop you had to have plenty of speed at the top otherwise you'd go into an inverted spin, which was very difficult, if possible, to get out of. So you went up until about 1944, up to the Mark 9, they were beautiful, lovely aircraft. And any airman could fly them, that goes for me too.

The last Spitfire I flew was in September 1945, and it was an F14, with its Griffon engine and clipped wing tips. It was a very formidable machine, but nothing like its original ladylike grace and charm. It was something that you just had to watch very carefully and I wasn't flying a great deal by that time and this type was new to me. As it happened I was flying down to Andover in Hampshire, which was still a little grass airfield at that time, sloping slightly downhill into the prevailing wind. And I had to land this horrible brick and I may tell you that before I was over the hedge and touched down I

Donald Jack, third from right, wearing mess dress kilt.

had the brakes full on. But I made it all right and by God, I wasn't happy at all. And that was my last flight in a Spitfire. I'd much rather it had been a Mark 1 or even a 9, the Mark 9 was the one that I liked best of all. And I was talking earlier on about always being under the 109, German 109 fighters. But the Mark 9, Rolls Royce had developed a second supercharger, so that when the power started to fall away about 27,000 feet, press a switch and in would come the second supercharger and off you could go for another 5,000 feet. And you could join issue with them then, greatly to the dismay of the 109 pilots who'd always had it their own way up at that height. So that's my history of Spitfires.

Looking back on the war, it was certainly momentous. But it was only just makeshift really, it prevented something happening. But it didn't, well I suppose it did have an ultimate effect on the war in that if he [Hitler] had invaded Britain the chances are that he might have invaded successfully. And it would have been far more difficult to launch D-Day landings in Normandy if we didn't have the platform of Britain. So I suppose it had an effect on the ultimate outcome of the war. But things were still going badly with the Allies. The first change in our fortunes that I know of was winning the El Alamein battle, because when I was out there... I just got out to Egypt at the time that Rommel was pushing right up and through the Egyptian frontier into Egypt and within a biscuit toss of Cairo and of course the wonderful ports of Port Said and Alexandria. From there, there would have been nothing stopping him from getting through to Iraq,

robbing us of all that Middle East oil, and through to India joining up with the Japs* and it could have been all over for us. But luckily, because of the distance of his supply lines he couldn't push any further than round about El Alamein until he got these ports in Egypt, Port Said and Alexandria. So we were able to consolidate and the army built up the requisite number of tanks, guns and so on, which put Rommel for the first and only time into retreat.

I left 602 just before Christmas 1940. I'd been in the squadron actively from September 1939 right to nearly the end of December 1940. So they reckoned that I could do with a little change of scene. So I got posted to a fighter group that covered the whole area of eastern Scotland and North East England, 13 (Fighter) Group. And I was made a staff officer and promoted to Squadron Leader, and that was great. I led a nine-to-five existence, which was marvellous. And no night flying interceptions, or anything like that. Brought my wife up to Newcastle; as it happened, it was my only experience of married life was that five months in Newcastle.

However, in the beginning of May, 13 Group was given three new fighter squadrons to form, and I was offered one of them. So I selected number 123 Squadron which was forming at Turnhouse. So I moved up there and we collected our aircraft, requisite number of pilots, which at that time was about 30. And all the airmen and all the trimmings – adjutant, intelligence officer, engineering officer, the lot. And we started training in earnest, mainly directed towards the offensive patrols from the south of England and they were really quite new to fighter command. I got some experience with joining the squadron down in the south to find out what it was really like and I came back and tried to teach my new pilots for the training.

As it happened, a lot of the pilots, as they became trained, were posted south to other squadrons in the south because the casualties were fairly heavy on these offensive patrols. So we were continually getting new pilots posted, training hindered slightly by the fact that HMS *Prince of Wales*, one of our escorts, came into Rosyth for a refit after its encounter with the *Bismarck* in the Atlantic. So we were moved to Drem and immediately adopted an operational role in that we were responsible for the defence of *Prince of Wales* while she was in harbour. That was a bit annoying because we always had to have six aircraft in readiness, so that only gave us another six to fly training. But however, that went on. We eventually got ourselves to what I thought was an efficient peak. Ready to be posted down south and take part in these offensive operations. But instead of that the squadron was posted away up to Castletown near Thurso, again for protection of the Navy at Scapa Flow. This was about February and we spent a miserable winter up there, very wild, terrible snowstorms, 90 miles an hour gales working through, escorting. We were told to prepare for going overseas, we did not know where.

So away we went, embarking at King George V Dock [Glasgow] just down the road and it was only half a mile away from where I had done my first solo in the Moth at Renfrew. And we went down the river, very nostalgic for us Glasgow boys, and lay off the Tail of the Bank for about three or four days and that was terrible because I had been very keen on climbing, hill climbing, sailing and so on whenever I could, and here we were locked up in this grotty ship and to crown it all, the bars did not open because we were not beyond the 12 miles limit so that added to our frustration and misery. However we set off and had a safe trip way across to South America then back south-eastwards again to Freetown in Sierra Leone and we took in water and stuff at Freetown and that was interesting. Then away down the Southern Atlantic. Blue, blue water, gorgeous like the older products of Stephens ink [a fountain pen ink], gorgeous colour and of course flying fish and dolphins round the Cape. We went far south of the Cape into green water to avoid Japanese submarines that hung about the sea routes at Cape Town and then back north again up to Durban where we spent about 10 days. Then on by Mauritania to Port Tewfik, Suez across to Cairo and the day after we arrived at Cairo.

We were all summoned to Air Chief Marshal Tedders' office, he was C-in-C Middle East at that time. There were six of us, there were six fighter squadrons sent overseas at the same time, two wings, so six Squadron Commanders who were interviewed by Tedder, who welcomed us very warmly, and said, 'Nice to see you buggers, but I am very sorry I have no aircraft for you. Unfortunately, they were being sent out by sea in crates on two cargo ships to Takoradi [Ghana] to be re-built and then flown across to Egypt, but sadly the ships were sunk'. So he said, 'If you leave it with me for a few days I will see what I can do', and true to his word we were sent to reinforce other fighter squadrons in the desert who had come back in the retreat, and a lot of them were in fairly bad shape and lost a lot of people, a lot of pilots, so we went there and reinforced these squadrons, six of the desert squadrons. It was a great experience, from my point of view, because they all had experienced and understanding squadron commanders. I was able to learn an awful lot.

I was in a Hurricane bomber squadron for a bit and that was very interesting, discovering my dive bomber techniques and so on. Then we were transferred to reinforce 80 Squadron, which was in bad shape and almost immediately I was posted to Command and 123 Squadron was dropped. It eventually went to the Far East, but I was given command of 80 Squadron and the first night I was there with my two Flight Commanders we chose the 30 best pilots from the original 80 and my 123 Squadron and that made our complement of pilots and we were off mainly patrolling over the Alamein line. Then, of course, in October the Alamein Battle and Montgomery won the Alamein Battle, and the Germans started retreating and we had a terrific time strafing the retreating columns, taking prisoners, mostly Italians. We took thousands of Italians prisoner. But anyway our roles [were] strafing and generally harassing the retreating Germans but being a Hurricane IIc squadron we did not get that far up the line. We dropped off at Tobruk and that was as far east that we went in that campaign, but we had a good time at Tobruk, interesting. So that was my career.

I eventually left 80 Squadron in February 1943 and was posted to Air Headquarters Middle East. I was given a job as a Staff Officer. My training at 13 Group away in 1941 was quite useful and I had a great time. My job was liaison with all the squadrons in the desert and I was given a Hurricane, an old Hurricane IIc, as my own aircraft. It was kept at Heliopolis, which was about 10 miles out of Cairo, and I could fly it whenever I wanted and I could go up and down, wonderful job. They wanted me because they wanted somebody who was not a wingless Staff Officer, they wanted somebody who could liaise with the squadrons, somebody who could talk in the language of the squadrons and they might, in these circumstances, do what was asked of them because there was an old saying in the RAF, 'An order was merely the basis for a discussion'.

When I was in my last year at school, I was really keen on playing rugger. In fact, my ambition really was I would have loved to have put on the blue jersey and played rugger for Scotland. But in one of the matches I had got my knee very badly smashed up playing in a match, as a result of which I had to have it operated on and then the surgeons afterwards said, 'Well, it should be fairly serviceable for you later on, but for goodness sake no more rugger'. That of course was a great disappointment to me.

So after I left school I thought, 'Well I'm not going to just spend my weekends watching rugger, I'll see about perhaps joining one of the Territorial Army units'. And I got a hold of a copy of the Glasgow Post Office Directory, at the back of which was a list of all the local units with the names of officers who were in them. And I thought, 'Well I'll glance through this and see which unit to join, perhaps one that had most friend of mine, old friends'. And right at the end I came across the 602 Squadron Auxiliary Air Force, and I had never heard of it before and I thought, 'This sounds rather interesting'. So I wrote to them and I was invited to go down to Abbotsinch, where they'd just recently moved, from Renfrew. And it so happened it was a stand-down weekend, and the only people who were there was the Commanding Officer and the Adjutant, the regular Adjutant.

The Commanding Officer at the time was the Marquis of Clydesdale and the Adjutant was a fellow called Stacey Hodson. And they treated me very kindly and I had a long chat with Lord Clydesdale and in the course of which he said, 'Have you done much flying?' I said, 'Sir, I have never been near an aeroplane before', and just then Hodson came into the room and Clydesdale said, 'Meet Johnstone, he has shown an interest in flying. You're just going to do an air test, I understand, in one of the training aircraft' – it was an Avro 504 – 'Why not take Johnstone up for a trip, he has never flown before?'. So I was kitted up and put in the back of this 504 and I think Hodson, realizing that this was my first trip, really put me through the mill. We spent our time, most of the time, upside down or doing aerobatics. My main worry – I was fairly enjoying it – my main worry was that my loose change might fall out of my pockets. But when we got back on the ground they invited me across to the mess for a cup of tea and it started from there. I was asked to go down the following weekend and meet the chaps who had been flying. And I was invited later on to our dining-in nights and so on. And then finally, and this was one of the nice things, I think, about most auxiliary squadrons, nobody was invited to join unless all the other chaps were anxious to have him in. So the net result, you had a very good and friendly team, and that's how I got started flying in the Auxiliaries.

I had no idea then that I would have a whole career in the Royal Air Force. When I left school, at first, I had joined an East India Merchants firm in Glasgow. And it was while I was there that I joined the Auxiliaries and I used to fly at the weekends with them. I later moved through to a job in Edinburgh, but I still travelled through at the weekends to fly with 602 Squadron. I was still Auxiliary right through the War and it wasn't until after the War that I put myself forward for a commission, a regular commission, in the Air Force.

My Flight Commander in the Squadron was David McIntyre. My CO was the Duke of Hamilton. And I always remember Mac coming up to me one day and saying, 'Douglo and I are going to start up an airfield down at Prestwick, a training school, and we were going to have a navigation site at it, and I know you are interested in navigation. Would you like to come and join us?'. And that's how I started flying commercially. I had to go through all the rigmarole of getting a B licence, commercial pilot's licence, and passing the various flying tests and so on. So I was flying commercially during the week at Prestwick and at the weekends, most weekends, coming up and flying with 602 Squadron at Abbotsinch. So I really was flying four to seven days a week at one point.

That was pretty much the pattern up until the start of the Second World War except I had a slight respite because, by that time, they made me the Chief Instructor at the VR School [Volunteer Reserve]. That meant I had to fly with them at the weekends, just for about the last two months before I was called up. But otherwise it was seven days a week for about two years non-stop.

By this time I had got bitten by the bug, to put it mildly. But we started, of course, when we were called up, at Abbotsinch. I always remember very early on, it was pretty uncomfortable I must say, we weren't allowed to sleep in the mess, we had to sleep in tents out beside our aircraft.

On the night of the 30th of September 1939 it was a thick fog, they should probably well remember it, it was either blowing a gale or thick fog in Glasgow. It was a thick fog night. So much so that they hadn't even bothered to lay out a flare path, because nobody's going to be mad enough to be expected to fly. But in the middle of the night (by this time I was in my pyjamas sleeping on my camp bed in the tent), the telephone went and I was ordered to take off. So all I could do was put on a greatcoat, pull on my trousers over my pyjamas to go outside, but I couldn't find the aircraft in the fog, eventually found it [and] started up. An airman ran in front of me with a torch. I followed him and he eventually shone it up at a windsock, so I knew where we were on the airfield.

So I took off by instruments and I never saw the ground again – quite frankly, from then on there was just solid fog. I thought, 'This is stupid, my radio didn't seem to work', all I got was some foreign dance music on it. Eventually, fortunately, I had a parachute flare fitted to the Spitfire. After a while I thought, 'This is ridiculous', I'd flown on towards Prestwick because I thought if it was going to be clearer anywhere it will be clear in that area, but it wasn't, it was still just a blanket. So I turned and came back on the reciprocal [a 180 degree turn] for about five minutes less than what I had already flown, 20 minutes one way and 15 minutes the other way. I started to let down a bit to about four or five thousand feet and pulled off my parachute flare.

Sandy Johnstone in front of his aeroplane after flying into the side of a hill near Lochwinnoch, 30th September 1939.

I could see that I was over open country and I thought, 'This is too good an opportunity'. Then I saw a huge field, I thought, and I pumped the wheels down, you had to pump the wheels in a Spitfire down. I was lining up on this thing with the flare spluttering above me, and I suddenly realized it wasn't a field, it was a reservoir I was aiming for! So I jammed the throttles open again, by which time the flare went out. I was left in the dark, still with the wheels up, I may say, which was fortunate, and then I slammed straight into the side of a hill. It was quite near Lochwinnoch [Renfrewshire]. And I slithered right up to the top of the hill and hit a stone cairn at the top of it, which whirled me round and gave me a bump on the head. And I must say I never got out of a Spitfire so quickly in my life because I was expecting it to blow up. But, by Jove, it was cold sitting up on the top of that hill in the beginning of October in one's pyjamas I can assure you. I eventually heard a noise and it sounded like a motor horn. I made my way up to that, and of course it was the undercarriage warning horn that was blaring away and that led me back to the aircraft. It was sufficiently undamaged for me to climb into the cockpit. But this horn was still going and I couldn't think how to stop it. I nearly broke my fingernails trying to get the cowlings off and then it suddenly dawned on me just to open the throttle. So eventually I sat up there shivering in the cold, and suddenly I was aware of a double-barrelled shotgun being pointed at me a voice saying, 'Who are you?'. And to be honest, I couldn't even remember my name, I was so scared, and I saw this double-barrelled shotgun. It had been the keeper of the reservoir who'd heard all this kerfuffle and thought I was a German,

and he had come up and he was pointing the gun. However, he rescued me and took me down to his house. I rang up Abbotsinch and Archie McKellar, I always remember Archie McKellar, drove out and picked me up. And that was my first operational patrol. I believe it was the first night operational patrol done by a Spitfire, but it wasn't a very successful one!

The Spitfire is a wonderful aeroplane, there is no doubt about it, and the more one flew it the more attached to it you became. I always reckoned that getting into a Spitfire, unlike any other aircraft I've flown, and I've got 107 different types I've flown, but unlike any other, it's rather like putting a jacket on; it fitted you. You got into this beautiful aeroplane, and the more you flew it you could always make it talk in the end. We were very fortunate in getting Spitfires I reckon.

The first operation in the Firth of Forth was interesting. By that time the Squadron had moved from Abbotsinch over to the east coast at Drem. One of our main jobs was providing air cover for the coastal convoys as they went south, sailing out of Methil Bay on the Firth of Forth and down the east coast. This particular day there seemed to be an undue amount of traffic, other traffic, and people were being sent in all different directions for no particular purpose. And it so happened that I had taken over the flight, Douglas Farquhar here was leading the section of three aircraft. But his radio went u/s [unserviceable] so he signalled to me to take over the flight. We had been getting rather short of fuel for a while. And I suddenly realized that there was a very strong southerly wind against us and it was going to be dicey to get back to Drem, although I could see it in the distance. So I landed the three lads at Leuchars to refuel, and they said, 'You'd better go and have some lunch'. So I went across to the mess and it was while we were sitting having lunch in the mess that we heard the sirens go off. Everybody dashed out including us, and then we sat, because the air-raid shelters were full up, so we just sat on top. And I remember Douglas Farquhar looking up and saying, 'Oh look, there's some Blenheims'. And I looked up and he said, 'Hang on a minute'. And he went off and came rushing back in immediately, phoned up Turnhouse and said, 'Gosh, those weren't Blenheims, they were Heinkels, come on!' [they were in fact JU88s]. So he's raced up, by which time the chaps up in Leuchars had got our aircraft going, and we took off. Of course by the time we got to the Forth Bridge most of the trouble was over, the chaps had gotten in amongst them. But we didn't. My only contribution to that effort was a long range shot at a Heinkel disappearing into a cloud. I still thought it looked like a Blenheim, I must confess. That was my first, what you might say operational, real operational sortie – again not very successful.

The Squadron was based at Drem for quite a long while from October 1939, apart from one spell we moved up to Dyce, Aberdeen, to cover the withdrawals of the troops from Norway. Then they came back to Drem again. And we did most of our operational flying from there, as I say, providing protection for the convoys. But as well as that we actually shot down 19 aircraft while we were still up there. Before the Battle of Britain the Squadron's total was up to 19 and then things began to hot up. We very nearly went down to cover the Dunkirk evacuation, but in fact an aircraft had come up, a heavy aircraft and all our stuff had been loaded on board, and then the order came to cancel it because it was finished.

A matter of weeks afterwards we were told we were going down to the Battle of Britain, which was getting underway. And we, as a squadron, flew down to Westhampnett, which was the satellite airfield of Tangmere. It's very rudimentary, this satellite airfield. It had just recently been put into effect – it was just really three fields that had been knocked into one; they had taken the hedgerows down. There were no buildings, two Nissen huts, I think, and a windsock. That was all, this is what we landed down there with. And we were the only Spitfire Squadron in the sector, the other two squadrons at Tangmere were Hurricanes. So we had no spares for the Spitfires. I always remember ringing up the station commander at Middle Wallop, who had a Spitfire Squadron there, and asking him if there was any chance of getting some spares off him. He said, 'Easy, old boy, send a lorry up and I'll see what we can do for you'. So the lorry went up and just arrived there before West Middle Wallop was bombed, of course things were chaotic. So the boys in it, led by a real old Glasgow corporal, marched into the stores and picked up what they wanted, drove the lorry up and drove out and came back with enough stuff to build a Spitfire, including an engine. So that's how we got going, and, bit by bit, our own spares were flown down and it became more sophisticated. But the first week was pretty hairy because Tangmere was bombed two days after we arrived there.

I don't think the Germans knew about Westhampnett, it was only three miles from Tangmere. We were scared of a direct raid most of the time, Tangmere got pretty badly pasted. So we got involved in that. That was really the first big action we were involved in after we got down south – when Tangmere was bombed. We were all sitting having our lunch and we were suddenly told to scramble. Normally we were put to a state of what they called readiness, which was usual, but this, we were released at this point. The chaps just tore down across into the airfield, got into the aircraft, took off from all directions, how nobody collided, I don't know how! I think Findlay Boyd, one of my flight commanders, he was taking off and a Stuka had just come down right in front of him as he was taking off. And he was so shaken that he just let fly at it and shot it down in front of him and he was so shaken he just completed his circuit and landed again. He never even pulled his wheels up and he'd already shot one down. Talk about chaos, that's what it was.

It's very difficult to give you an accurate picture of what it was like during the Battle of Britain itself. I think the main thing was that one got very tired. You were sitting at the end of the telephone, that's the only time one was apprehensive. Once the order to scramble came, everybody was too busy to get frightened or anything else. But, you were racing up to 15–20,000 feet or over, down again, up again, down again, it was very tiring. It was not unusual to find chaps coming out of their aircraft, sitting down on their wooden chair and falling fast asleep. I think that tiredness is the thing that I remember more than anything, the exhaustion. Never any fears, never any question of being frightened. It was nasty seeing chaps going down, it was nasty seeing Germans going down, quite frankly. It was rather funny later on, I got to know one of the Germans we used to fight against, who had commanded a Messerschmidt 109 Squadron in Northern France. And when we met Mackie Steinhoff [Johannes Steinhoff, later to be General of the Luftwaffe], we compared notes and discovered that we'd been in at least three actions together. Because, fortunately he spoke very good English. I'll always remember him saying, 'By gosh you know, we're ruddy awful shots, aren't we, we're both still alive'. But of course that was after the war.

It was frenetic at times, very frenetic and at other times it was boring, you were sitting on the ground waiting, that was when one got apprehensive. The civilian population were absolutely marvellous. This is why I feel myself that everybody was pulling together, everybody, I don't mean just the service, people living round about us. I remember the Duke of Richmond came and called on me because we were out by Goodwood [his estate in West Sussex]. That was very nice of him. And he said, 'Have you any particular problems?' I said, 'Well, we've got nowhere to put our stores'. And I always remember him saying, 'Well now, I don't think the racing calendar is going to be much use to us this year, why not use the grandstand up at Goodwood race course?' So that's what we used, we moved into the grandstand for our equipment section.

Then of course there was the problem of nearly a half-mile walk up to it from the airfield and the chaps' shoes kept wearing out, so we had to get a bus. It so happened that the Duke of Kent was visiting some stations and he heard that we wanted this bus. So he told the station commander at Tangmere to get a bus. Now his way of dealing with it was to send his squadron leader admin up to the main road, stop the first south-bound double-decker bus that came along, turned the passengers out, wrote a wee chit, gave it to the driver – we'd taken a corporal driver of our own, he climbed in, run up 'Special' [as the destination] and drove off and we had the bus for the rest of the time we were there. It was great, nobody complained. At that time even after the bombing of London started …the spirit these people… I mean it was an inspiration to us – if they can stand it, we can stand it. I reckon this country was never in a healthier state than it was at that time, in spite of everything, everybody was working towards the same end.

We weren't aware of the critical nature of the situation that Britain was in, quite honestly. As I said before, we'd been doing a lot of flying up at Drem, we'd already shot about 19 down before we came south. So what we were doing really, was a continuation at a greater level of what we were doing up north. And it wasn't, quite frankly, until Churchill made his famous remark about 'Never in the field of human…', people looked at one another and said, 'Who's he talking about?'. I said, 'Gosh, that's us'. We weren't aware, we realized it was very serious particularly when the threat of invasion was still very much on everybody's minds

and we hated it when a southerly wind came because we expected to be besieged by gas, you see. So one hung onto one's gas mask very thoroughly and everything that could be painted with that special paint that showed up gas was painted. I probably was one of the worst shots in the squadron. I couldn't hit the back end of a cow with a frying pan. But there were so many Germans that if you fired in their general direction you generally hit something. I was credited with, I think it was eight confirmed victories and four probables, and oh, a hell of a lot more were scared stiff I may say, I hope!

At the end of the Battle of Britain, 602 was the longest serving squadron of all down in the south. We went on the 13th of August and stayed there till the 19th or the 20th of December. So we moved on to Prestwick at that point, and, once there, of course, we realized that practically all the original chaps were either dead or had moved to other squadrons or been promoted. It was really starting with a fresh squadron again, building up another squadron. During the course of that one I was told I was moving to become Station Commander, Fighter Control at Turnhouse, where my old friend the Marquis of Clydesdale, who'd then become the Duke of Hamilton, was the Commanding Officer. It so happened that the night, or the night after, I'd got over there, gone up to have dinner with the Duke and his Duchess up in the house, Milburn House or Milburn Towers I think it's called, when Hess arrived. Douglo was called to the telephone and when he came back he said, 'There's a chap come, landed, a German, says he wants to see me and his name is Alfred Horn. I don't know anybody Alfred Horn'. But the intelligence people seemed to think there was something on, so Douglo went off to Glasgow where they had taken him, into Maryhill Barracks, he'd landed at Eaglesham. I went back to Turnhouse, to the Ops room and about one o'clock in the morning the Duke of Hamilton then came in and took me into the rest room, and I thought he looked very agitated and he shut the door, I always remember him locking the door, and shutting the ventilators. I thought, 'My goodness', and he said, 'Don't think I'm mad, but I think Rudolph Hess is in Glasgow'. I was probably the second person to hear this, he never let on to the people who had taken him through to Glasgow. I reckon I was number two to hear about it.

While I was at Prestwick, just before I left the squadron, the well-known blitz on Clydeside happened. We were sent up, among others, to try and deal with it. But they were going to try a new system called Fighter Night that meant stacking the aircraft one on top of the other at 500-feet intervals. And the ack-ack guns were given freedom of range up to 12,000 feet. So it literally was a theoretical space of 2,000 feet between. Now, we never could prove it, but that's the space at which the Germans came in and dropped their bombs. Now I actually saw the silhouette of two Heinkels, I was about 15,000 feet up, well down below me. But I daren't leave my position because the others were circling below me. It was a disaster, it was the only time it was ever tried, it was very unfortunate it happened over Glasgow, particularly for us Glaswegians knowing that our loved ones were down below. That was one of the less fortunate incidents in which the 602 was involved, it was no fault of ours that it didn't come off.

I was posted to the Middle East in 1941. So I said, 'Well' – incidentally the signal said 'Wanted urgently' – so I said, 'Well, give me an aircraft and I'll fly it out'. They said, 'No no, just you follow your instructions'. In the long run it took two and a half months to get out there, by the time I got into a convoy and sailed across to America and round South Africa and everything. When I got out there I was posted up to Beirut. It was rather funny actually, because when I turned up at the headquarters in the Middle East which was in Cairo, the Senior Personnel Staff Officer [SPS] said, 'Who are you?' I said, 'Well, here's my signal I'm wanted urgently'. 'Never heard of you', he said, 'What've you been doing?' I said, 'Well I've been a fighter controller at Turnhouse'. 'Oh, excellent! We're just looking for some fighter controllers out in the Western Desert'. So my heart sank, I had visions of being boxed up in a box out in the Western Desert, but couldn't argue. And as I left the SPS said to me, 'By the way Johnstone, do you speak French?', I said, 'Yes, fluently', he said, 'Oh that's right, you better go to Beirut'. I couldn't speak a bloody word of the language but neither could he, which was very fortunate! So I learned how to speak French when I got up to Beirut, I was posted as a Squadron Leader Ops, up at the headquarters there, which was really just forming. We'd just got rid of the Free French, and it was all slightly chaotic.

At the end of 1941, they discovered that I'd been promoted to Wing Commander on 1st of January but I didn't get the message till late on in February. And they said, 'Well, we haven't got space for a Wing Commander here'. So I went down to Haifa Station Commander. It was while I was there that I'd been down at headquarters again and flown back with the C-in-C [Commander in Charge], who was Lord Tedder, he flew me back in his aircraft. We were having lunch together and I happened to mention to him, 'Any chance of getting back onto operational flying again?' He said, 'I don't think so, but we'll see what we can do'. And bless his heart, about 10 days later I had a signal from him saying, 'I've got you a wing of Spitfires in Malta, find your own way there'. And it took me

about two weeks to eventually get an aircraft that was going out. I think the total payload, of a Liberator it was, was a General who'd been on leave, myself, a naval torpedo, and sacks of dehydrated potatoes. That was the load that I arrived with in Malta, in the middle of a raid I may say. But I didn't take over the wing immediately because I'd taken so long to get there that the AOC [Air Officer Commanding] who, incidentally was Keith Park, who'd also been my OC [Officer Commanding] during the Battle of Britain said, 'I really couldn't wait', so he'd given my wing to somebody else. They said, 'You'll get the next one that comes up'. So for a while I acted as Deputy Station Commander at

'A' Flight, 602 Squadron, Drem 1940. From left to right, back row: Flying Officer Coverley, Flying Officer Webb, Flying Officer Jack, Warrant Officer McIntosh, Flying Officer Grant, Flying Officer McKellar, Flying Officer Ferguson and Flying Officer Ritchie. Front row: Flight Lieutenant Urie, Flight Lieutenant Robinson, Flight Lieutenant Farquhar, Flight Lieutenant Johnstone and Flight Lieutenant Boyd.

Luqa, and plotted all the bombs as they came down. Then I got my wing, the Ta Kali wing that moved to Crendi which was an airfield that had just opened. And blow me down, I was just getting under way there when I went down with Malta fever. So that meant I had to be sent home.

I was taken off flying for a bit and they sent me to the staff college that was then at Gerrard's Cross, at Bulstrode Park. Strangely enough, one of my fellow students, whom I became very friendly with, was a certain Wing Commander Frank Whittle, the chap who'd just invented the jet engine – nobody knew about them. He gave us a lecture, while we were at the staff college, in the greatest secrecy. And that's the first any of us heard ever about jet engines, and in fact he brought the original jet engine itself, got it sent down and ran it up in the grounds of the staff college. This was in 1943. It was a good six months before it became generally known that we had jets.

Well, having more or less survived the war up to this point, when I left the staff college I got back onto flying. I regained my flying category, and went up to Tealing, which is an airfield just north of Dundee, as a Wing Commander flying at a Hurricane OCU [Operational Conversion Unit]. I wasn't there very long before I was posted down to take command of a sector down in South Wales, in Fairwood Common. I was there for, oh, six, seven months. I remember the C-in-C and the AOC, the C-in-C was Roderick Hill and the AOC was Charles Steele. They came down to see me one day, they were going round actually giving lectures to the chaps, there'd been a lot of taxiing accidents. They were saying, you know, 'Anymore of this and you'll be out on your ear'. I'll never forget it, I went down to see them off in the course of which he said, 'By the way, how do you get on with Leigh-Mallory? [the Air Chief Marshal]. Because that's where you're going next'. But when I went to see the AOC and the C-in-C off, one flying a Spitfire the other flying a Hurricane, they collided on the ground and I thought this is marvellous, we never heard another thing about it.

From there I went up and joined Leigh-Mallory as his Group Captain Ops, about three weeks before D-Day. We saw that through, very interesting I must say. But when Eisenhower moved his headquarters across to France, by that time Leigh-Mallory knew that he was going out to the Far East and he didn't want to go so I was sent over in his place. I worked very closely with Eisenhower for quite a period, got to know him well. He, in fact, sent me over to America, to a course, where I was met by Mrs Eisenhower, put up for a weekend there, and I had a great time. Before I went to America of course, I'd gone to see Leigh-Mallory and his wife off on their trip and that was when they crashed, they didn't... I was probably one of the last people to see them. So, that was it.

Now, I was still in America doing this course, we spent a month at the Air College in Florida. Then I spent a week with the School of Infantry in Oklahoma, and another one in Georgia. And then we went to the Army Staff College at Kansas for a month. Then moved on into the Naval College. And with that background we went into the Planning Department in Washington for three months and while I was at Rhode Island, VE day happened. I came back, sailed back on the *Queen Mary* incidentally, great style on the boat deck with a communicating door into the next cabin with Bob Hope and Gerry Colona in it. Between us we had 28 bottles of whisky so we did very well on the trip back.

Then when I got back, shortly afterwards, VJ day occurred and I was then a Deputy Assessor at 12 Group, which was in the Midlands near Nottingham. From there I went to Malaya where I actually founded the Royal Malayan Air Force, from scratch, which was rather fun. I became known as the father of the Royal Malayan Air Force and so on. When I came back from that, they'd made me an Air Commodore by this time, when I came back from that I dropped this Air Commodore rank for one more tour. I became Station Commander at a big fighter station near Middlesborough, at Middleton St George. I was promoted to Air Commodore, then after the end of that job I was sent up to the Imperial Defence College in London, I did a year at that. At the end of which I became the Director of Personnel at the Air Ministry. Following which I went out to Borneo to run the air side of the air war between the Malays and the Indonesians. And after that I was promoted yet further, I don't know how I got promoted, to Air Vice Marshal and ended up as Air Officer Scotland where I'd begun. It was nice, I enjoyed it all.

After the war of course the auxiliary squadrons were disbanded as a whole and then they resuscitated them for a while, which I was very pleased about. I was also invited at that time by the Duke of Norfolk to become his deputy in the TAVR, the Territorial and Voluntary Reserves, in London. I took that on for 10 years, during which we did our best to get the auxiliaries properly going. They didn't come out flying again for a short time but they just put their foot down and said, 'No more flying'. But they did get them going in relation to the ground defence side of the business and the fighter control side. But long after I'd left the Air Force the proposition came up about what had been one of the gate guardians, a Spitfire sitting outside Leuchars which was an ex post-war 602 Squadron Spitfire, and we were offered it for the 602 Squadron Museum. In fact, I corresponded with Michael Portillo about this, and said we'd be delighted to have it, but of course it was much too large to go inside our own museum. Of course I had nothing to do with it but I was delighted to hear that the City of Glasgow were going to accept it into the Art Galleries, where I hope it will remain forever. I am delighted I must say, it's not an aircraft I was personally concerned with because it came into the squadron after the war, and after it had been disbanded and restarted again. I think Marcus Robinson was the first CO after the war, during that period.

The Spitfire played an enormous role in the Second World War. Particularly, strangely enough, to the Germans – I mentioned Mackie Steinhoff – he taught me that it was infra dig for a German to be shot down by a Hurricane. Whether it was a Hurricane or not they said, 'It was a Spitfire, it was a Spitfire'. They were frightened of the Spitfires, they thought they were very good aeroplanes. I agree with them.

I joined the Air Force in 1940 when I was 19, and after years of messing around, I went to train as a pilot in Rhodesia and I trained on Tiger Moths and Harvards and then I came back to this country, which was unusual, there weren't very many of them [pilots] came back, most of them went up to the Middle East. I came back to this country and my initial work was involved with the early days of military gliders and we flew some of the early gliders and we towed them with Harts and Hinds, which were the old pre-war bi-planes. After I'd done that for a bit I went on to Spitfires and I was trained at Grangemouth in Scotland and Balado Bridge where we did our advanced air gunnery and so forth. After that I was posted to 277 Squadron on the south coast, which was an Air Sea Rescue Squadron and they flew Spitfire 5s down there. The basic work was Air Sea Rescue right down on the French coast there and we actually operated a dual role. Mostly to protect our own people and also as a reconnaissance. We had to look for people in water and those particular Spitfires had a dinghy inserted behind the pilot's seat which could drop the people in the water a Mae West. I was there for a year and a half I suppose, and after D-Day when our service was not required to the same extent, I left there and I went onto Typhoons, coming right up until the end of the war and we finished up at the end of the war, right behind where the peace was signed and then went onto Denmark. After that we spent a few months in Germany and then because we were all really tour expired at that time, we didn't go out to the Far East and I came back to this country and went back on

Spitfires again with Fighter Affiliation Coastal Command this time. We were flying Spitfire 16s with Packard Merlins and we were down in South Devon and I was there until I was de-mobilized. About a year later 602 Squadron was re-formed in Glasgow under Marcus Robinson and I joined there. I was back in Spitfires again for the third time and I stayed with the 602 Squadron when they moved from Spitfires to the early jets. We were called up during the Korean War for a short time and shortly after that I took over the Squadron as Squadron Leader and I was in that capacity for a while. Then my Company sent me out to the Middle East so I had to give up flying, took something to work for my living after that.

I started flying at Grangemouth. It was all very exciting, I terribly wanted a go on a Spitfire, I mean they were a legend at that time, everybody wanted them. We trained on the Spitfires which had the pump undercarriage, you know, to pump the undercarriage up, and the only time that I ever had engine problems was my second flight on a Spitfire from Grangemouth when the engine stopped. And I had a crash land, at Slamannan, and I landed on a peat bog there, and I put the propeller into coarse, which meant the propeller feathered, went into the peat bog and I didn't even break the propeller. So it gave me great confidence in the aircraft. I flew about another 570 hours on Spitfires after that, but I never had another engine failure. I reckoned we had got a really good aircraft there.

The aircraft was a natural, it was a very tight aircraft, and I felt very much part of the aircraft. It was so tight, in fact, that when you had an oxygen mask on and you turned your head to the left or right you would actually hit the canopy, unless you sort of withdrew your head a bit, and it was very tight all round, not like some of the other aircraft, where you could get up and walk around the cockpit. It was a very, I don't know how to put it, you felt at one with aircraft right from the word go.

It's the only aircraft I felt that I was really part of the aircraft, all the others I was sitting at doing something. But the Spitfire always felt as if it was moulded round you. They didn't suit very big people, I may say. But that was the feeling you got, that you were very much a part of the thing.

We had two cannons and four machine guns, as opposed to the older models which had eight machine guns, and although it had a lot more punch, I never actually took to the cannon because they nearly always let me down in critical moments. I shot down a V1 in a Mark 5 which was a bit unusual, and once again the cannon packed up when I opened fire so I had to finish off the job with the machine gun and I have mixed experiences with cannon on Typhoons which also tended to let me down at odd moments. They were useful weapons but they had their drawbacks.

We were going on patrol along the south coast towards Beachy Head and these V1s were coming over fairly thick and fast and the Spitfire 5 was not reckoned to be able to catch them, in fact one of the leading lights in those days wanted everybody forbidden to attack V1s unless they were in a Meteor or a Tempest because they reckoned they couldn't catch them. But we were told by control, there was one approaching and, blow me down, the thing appeared about 1500 feet below me just in the right position so I was able to put the nose down and get a bit of extra speed. So, I went after this thing and as I say when I opened fire the cannon stopped after about three rounds, and I had to go through the gate. If you're on the throttle you've got to have a little wire that can bridge, like override, and I was able to catch this thing, just, and, about 100 yards away, I looked up with the machine guns and the thing blew up and I went right through a fire ball, it was all very exciting. But everybody was shooting the things down but not very many people did it in 5s because they reckoned they weren't fast enough. Our top speed I suppose would be somewhere about, well 260, 280 perhaps. And these things could do up to about 500 miles per hour, so it was purely chance I had enough height to give it the extra speed to catch the thing up. But it was something excellent.

I think the most interesting part in those days was seeing D-Day. I saw D-Day from the air and it was something I will remember as long as I live. You see all these naval vessel ships, and all the rest of them coming all the way from Dover on one side and from Portsmouth to the other. They sort of joined up round about the Southampton area and headed across to Normandy and it was a sight that I don't think will ever be seen again, I

can, if I close my eyes, I can see it. Yes, the most extraordinary thing, tremendous effort by so many people.

I don't think I recall feeling particularly special because from our point of view flying Spitfires at that time, as the war tended to fade out, it was moving away from the UK into the Continent and the war was leaving, we could all sort of sit back and relax after a while, but there was all kinds of excitements.

Going to 602 was an ambition I had always had, being born in Glasgow, I'd always wanted to be in the Glasgow Squadron. Funnily enough, when our course from Grangemouth broke up, quite a few of our people did go to Glasgow, but I wasn't one of them. Anyway it was coming home at last and of course we were back in Spitfires again so it was great to be back on them again. It was a different scene all together of course, because there was no war going on, and you could really enjoy yourself because I was left doing the thing I liked most and that was flying. People who fly will know what I'm talking about. There is nothing greater than the sensation of flying, and in things like Spitfires it was great fun. And there was no worrying about enemy aircraft or flak or any of this sort of stuff. It was purely enjoyable, and it was great to be back, particularly up in Scotland, because I hadn't seen much of Scotland during the war apart from a very brief time at Grangemouth. The only problem was that of course, Scotland always got the worst of the equipment and the homing devices and means of getting you back at that time in bad weather, particularly on the fields around Glasgow, was a bit hazardous at times. But then we didn't take the risks that we would have done in wartime, we didn't really fly in very bad weather or anything of that sort. So it was good times, but it was fun then, not work.

We had Spitfires 21s and 22s. We had a mixture of both of them on the Squadron, and I suppose I flew them for two or three years before we went onto jets. One year we went to Summer Camp, it coincided with the fortieth Anniversary of Blériot crossing the Channel, and for reasons which I do not know, 602 Squadron was sent to Le Touquet to represent the Royal Air Force at this auspicious occasion and about half of our officers went over to Le Touquet in our Spitfires to take part in the celebration, mainly a French Air Force thing and we all went with the hope of a tremendous party which, I may say we did, and we got there and had a very good lunch and there were speeches by Madame Blériot and Lord Brabazon and French Air Force people. One of the things, incidentally, that intrigued me was that although I'm not a great French scholar, we got on very well with the French pilots because technical terms for flying were the same in both languages, so we were able to converse about Spitfires or whatever, with no difficulty at all. Anyway we had a very good lunch there and it was then announced, much to our surprise, that one of the 602 pilots was giving an aerial demonstration, we weren't quite prepared for that so we all looked round and Marcus Robinson decided that the person who should do the demonstration was he whose Spitfire had the most petrol in the tank, because in those days they were not allowed to refuel in France – it was to do with

the exchange rate of a pound and the franc and all that financial trouble. So all the tanks were dipped, the fullest tank was mine, so I gave a suitable demonstration about which I was a little nervous, having had a very good lunch, shall we say!

The Mark 21 wasn't so nice to fly, it was a heavier aircraft, and Spitfires were getting bigger all the time, it had a bigger engine, it was bigger all round and heavier and it didn't feel so manoeuvrable. And if I look back on all the various Marks I flew, I would say the 16 was one of the nicest because it was a lighter aircraft. It had clipped wings and particularly at low levels had a very high rate of roll and was far nicer to handle nearer the ground than say a 21. On the other hand they were designed for high level. What I said earlier on about the Spitfire being a multi-role aircraft, is that some people would work at low level doing ground attack, some medium level doing dive bombing, others would be at high level doing anti-fighter, anti-bomber work and the Spitfire was so versatile that it could cope with all these different aspects of flight. But they did very well with the Spitfire 21 to high level, much more so that, I would say, near the ground.

I'd encountered the thing [LA198] in between when it was stuck on a post at Leuchars in Fife. A sad end for the Spitfire. So, I'm very glad it is to be restored, if they put it back exactly as it was, people will be able to look at the thing in 50,100 years' time and say that's what it was. It's sort of come back to its natural home, after a very chequered career, and I think it's a great thing that it's coming back to Glasgow, and that it's going to take pride of place in Kelvingrove Museum.

It's certainly got a tale to tell to aircraft designers because the thing was conceived in 1935 and first flew in '36 and yet they were still flying the Mark 24s, still flying as late as 1955, and they kept improving the thing all the time. This was one of the things I found having flown about seven different marks I think, every one I flew was just that little bit better on improvements than the one before. I said earlier on, the first one I flew you had to pump the undercarriage up by hand. The early ones had a throttle, a mixture control and a pitch control. The next ones had a throttle and a pitch control. The mixture was regulated automatically and the final one had a throttle only. Everything was done not by computer but it was all done automatically. The pilot had less to think about working the machine or working the machinery and getting on with what he was supposed to be doing outside.

The first thing that any Spitfire pilot will notice is the huge nose in front of them, when you're sitting on the ground and the nose is up in front of you. You can see nothing in front of you. The best way I can describe it is, it's like driving a car with the bonnet up, you could only look out the side. So you have to turn the aircraft if you're taxiing; first one way and then the other so that you can look around the side. The other thing that was always drummed into us was that the brakes weren't of any help. They were only 30 per cent efficient; now the reason for this was that when you landed of course, you couldn't jam on your brakes and put the thing up on its nose, but they also have difficulties in that it

wasn't all that easy to taxi, because the brakes faded very quickly. The other feature on the ground of course was that there were very small radiators or one radiator in the early ones, two radiators in the later ones, like LA198, and they were great when you were going a couple of hundred miles an hour but when you had no air flow going through the radiators on the ground, you had roughly three minutes before your engine boiled and although you had glycol on the engine to raise the boiling temperature to about 120, three minutes wasn't all that long before you'd got to stop the engine and let the thing cool down. So that was another added feature. But once you got the things into the air, everything fell into place. You had aircraft that performed absolutely beautifully and were very forgiving, they didn't drop out of the sky when you stalled them, in fact even to get them into a spin was quite a difficult thing. They were very stable, they were very easy to come in and land, once you got rid of this business of not being able to see what was happening in front of you. But, I think the great thing was that it was a well-designed aircraft and had boundless possibilities and while a lot of aircraft maybe lasted for six months and they decided they were no use, the Spitfire was constantly modified. The original design was so good you could keep increasing the engine power, the wing span and so on and everybody was delighted with the thing.

First of all you had to start the engine, and my memory may be wrong here but I think LA198 had a thing called a Coffman starter. You didn't have a big electric battery to plug in, it was a thing like a shotgun cartridge that you pushed the button and that fired and started the engine. Now Spitfire engines were very easy to start, unlike some aircraft that were very dodgy. They started very easily and as soon as you got it started you checked you had your air pressure for your brakes, your oil pressure temperature, went through your pre-cockpit drill, make sure your trim was correct and then you taxied out to where you were going to take off from as quickly as possible before the thing boiled. When you were lined up on the runway you couldn't of course see what was in front of you but you could see down the side of the runway to known where you were going. You would make sure your pitch was fully fine and you would gradually open the throttle. Now as you opened the throttle the tail would come up and due to the gyroscopic effect of the propeller on its axis of rotation, which may be a bit technical. When that happened you got a vicious swing one way or the other, on Merlins it was to the right, on Griffons it was to the left, and you had to be prepared to catch this as the tail came up because otherwise the aircraft would tend to swing off the runway and the 21 had a much bigger rudder than the older aircraft because it had a more powerful engine, more torque, more tendency to swing, bigger rudder to counteract the swing and so on. Once you got the rudder up, then you could see what was happening ahead and round about 90 knots or so you'd have enough speed to gradually pull the stick back and the aircraft would just float off the ground. As soon as that happened you applied your brakes to stop the wheels spinning round and then one of the great tricks of Spitfires, you had to change hands because the undercarriage lever was on the right and you normally had your right hand on the stick so you had to make

sure your throttle didn't slip back, change left hand onto the stick, right hand to the rudder and raise your undercarriage with that. It became completely automatic, how you got your wheels up, you would then close your hood because most took off with their hood open. Partly for safety, if anything went wrong and you had to get out in a hurry, and also it gave you that little extra leeway to be able to stick your head out the side and look around to see what was happening. After that was a matter of building up climbing speed and carrying on to wherever you were going.

It was not a glamorous job, particularly with this war in Bosnia and Kosovo and all the rest of it, people tend to forget that war involves casualties and one of the sad things about that is that you tend to lose your friends. One of the reasons why a lot of people think it's a bad thing to have a crew of these squadrons flying as a unit is because they are all close friends and one thing I did learn during my career was that it's not a good thing to have close friendly relations with people during the war because they tend to disappear. The Second World War and the First World War had a lot in common in that we lost a lot of pilots and they were always the ones who just joined the squadron before they got experience and it was a well known saying that if you got to know their Christian name then they had a good chance of staying with you. It was not a glamorous job, it was a nasty job, on operations you lost a lot of people, you lost a lot of sleep and it was hard work. But the flying was great. And if you want a funny story about a Spitfire then I'll tell you one.

Just before D-Day there was a lot of deception going on, as you're probably aware, to confuse the enemy. On our particular airfield they decided to put in a dummy squadron. Now we had just been awarded the honour of having an [air] traffic control unit arrive and before that we just did our own thing and went off when we felt like it. But we had an air traffic control couple posted to us to tell us what to do and we didn't like it very much and just shortly after they arrived, this dummy squadron of Spitfires appeared and they put the first one up at the far end of the runway and they blew it up, it was an India rubber thing and they pumped it up with a foot pump so we waited watching this with great interest until it got one wing up and one wing on the ground and then we phoned up the air traffic control and said, 'Why don't you boys wake up? Don't you see that thing that's crashed at the end of the runway?' So they looked out the little window and saw this thing at the far end and they scrambled the fire tender and ambulance and we were absolutely delighted to see them. Ambulance and fire tender whiz up to the thing at high speed and about five minutes later they came slowly back. We could almost see their tails between their legs when they discovered it was only a rubber dummy. That fairly made our day.

Left to right: Alex Bowman, Jack Forrest and Jim Johnston welcoming LA198 back to Glasgow in April 1998.

I joined up in 1939, to get there and be excited with flying. I wanted to be wherever I could fly. I think that was fairly common too. We – those who joined up – didn't get political. I think I probably wanted to get away from medicine too. Other than that, away from home, all these exciting things, you know, meeting women and seeing the world. It worked too!

The RAF wouldn't have me as a pilot. I started as a wireless operator/air gunner. Looking back on it, I'm not surprised they wouldn't take me for a pilot first time around. I think the board were looking for men of good background with all the social graces. I was tremendously impressed by the Glasgow kids, impressed by how good and how self-confident and, in fact, superior, the public school boys were. The very, very first time we were all decanted from lorries, a couple of vans, in Warrington I think it was, and somebody said 'Now we need somebody to collect you shower'. Every Scot, and most of the others, cringed back. But, no, no, a voice piped up, 'I'll do it, OK, right chaps'. And I thought that is something that was not present in Scottish education, certainly not in Hyndland or Whitehill anyway. I've got to admire that self-confidence.

When I flew in flying boats my skipper was a chap called Toby O'Leary who died not very long ago. He was from near aristocracy – Eton, Oxford, beautiful manners, full of self-confidence. Something to admire, not a snob in any way. When I applied I was so green, I mean I was brought up largely by my mother in Athole Gardens

Left to right: Johnny MacGuire, Alex Richardson, and Jack Forrest.

[Glasgow], and I'd only got rid of shorts for about six months or so. It was a big, big world. I mean the first time you get searching questions like 'How high do you think this room is?' Who cares, you know? But in actual fact the questions were pertinent. The answers were circulating after I failed that time, so I got the answers. The next time I stood up to attention until asked to sit down. And the same question, 'How high would you say this room is?'. 'I would answer, '12ft 10 and a half inches, Sir!'. 'Good lad!' The unfortunate thing is, well in a way fortunate, but before the results were on the board, I'd been posted to Gib, Gibraltar. I trained up in Edmonton [Canada] and down in Stranraer in ancient flying boats. I went out to Gibraltar in 1940/41, we were virtually another leg of the Royal Navy. I was in things called Saro Londons, old bi-planes, lovely old things, and then Catalinas. My results didn't catch up with me for about a year. It was a lovely year; I enjoyed being in flying boats. In the middle of all that my pilot's course came through. I had another interview a month later, but they had to chase me around. And that was lovely, I went across on my own up to Bombay, stayed there for a few months, across to Durban, then up to Rhodesia; it was a lovely war. And I qualified as a pilot, came back to this country, and eventually finished up on Mosquitos on Night Fighter Squadron. And that was it, got de-mobbed.

At the end of the war I became an architecture student. I started at university and jumped at the chance of something to do in the evenings and flying Spits too – that was wonderful. That was the first time I flew Spits, I had never flown a single engine fighter until

peacetime, which was really good planning. I joined 602 specifically out of love of flying, but you know also the excitement and getting away. 602 was the only squadron that was there, other than the City of Edinburgh one. Yes, I'd say it was, I mean it was wonderful to finish at the university and go down to Abottsinch and finish up on the Long Strand at Islay, I don't know if you know but you can land right down on the sand, and arranging for the hotel to come through with tea and sandwiches.

Never having flown a Spit until that time, it was hard to compare it to anything else because it was the only single engine fighter I had flown. I can only compare with a Mosquito. Well as I say, I can only compare it with a twin-engine fighter. Much, much more forgiving and aerobatic but not necessarily as fast.

It was exciting being on one's own, very often in the Mosquitos there were two people, not always, but the Spit was great, if a bit unforgiving. I think the earliest Spit, when you're doing aerobatics, the crucial factor, the limiting thing is blacking out. The aircraft was capable of much more violent manoeuvres than the pilot could stand or could then stand. I used to wonder about the early Spits. The earlier Spits which were slower, must be much more manoeuvrable, and that would have been something. That would have been ideal. But having flown the earlier Spits you would probably have thought of the Gladiators, which were the bi-planes before and which were entirely more manoeuvrable. As a fighting machine, not having done any fighting I might say, it certainly made a mess of a target when you pressed the button you know. So did the Mosquito. By a target I mean a tow target or a static target. I don't know that it was any better than a Hurricane or any other fighters. But like 602, the glamour of the Spitfire has come through, you know, as the years go past. Not the Hurricane, which I think bore the brunt or even the Mosquito or the Beaufighter. The Spit somehow catches people's imagination, it's probably the film about Mitchell I think [*First of the Few*]. It did not have a legendary status then, but neither did 602. That is something that has grown up from then on, and I think the media have a lot to answer for. There's nothing about it that made it a great aeroplane. I wouldn't say it was the best fighter in the world or the worst fighter. I can only judge what I see on television nowadays; I didn't fly any other fighters, single engine ones. But it certainly was nice to fly, it was very thrilling. But on the other hand when I got married I gave it up quite happily. Just like I gave up riding a motorbike. It's a phase.

I think it is a good ideal preserving this particular one. Good for Glasgow. Visitors to Glasgow will love it and those of us that flew them will come to see it.

Alex Richardson, Tangmere, July, 1948.

Jim Johnston in the cockpit.

When I was a boy I was always keen on flying, and I joined the Air Defence Cadet Corps, which was the Air Training Corps at that time, at Dyce Airfield [Aberdeen]. The airfield had a couple of planes owned by a chap called Gandar Dower, an Englishman who used to fly passengers to Orkney, a passenger plane, and the best recruit in the Air Defence Corps always got a trip if there was any spare seats. I'd made sure I was the best, so I had a few trips there and that way started my flying. I really enjoyed it. I didn't actually fly but as a passenger. But the pilot let me glance at the instruments over his head. So I was really enthralled. I really enjoyed it.

So, I joined the Royal Air Force in August 1940, I was 18 years old. I volunteered for aircrew duties with the purpose of being a pilot and I was lucky, I had some flying experience, not actually flying myself but as a passenger next to the pilot. It didn't make much difference to the Royal Air Force actually. I think it's dependent on how you talk about it – if you were keen enough. You had to be showing you were keen, you couldn't say 'I'd like to be a pilot'; you had to say 'I *want* to be a pilot'.

The first aeroplanes I flew were Tiger Moths. That was the trainer. That's a bi-plane; you've probably seen them. And, believe it or not, they were the worst aircraft to fly. Why they were picked for first flying, I don't know. So light, a wee gust of wind and they were all over the place. But I enjoyed it very much.

We did six weeks training first of all ITW [Initial Training Wing], did ground duties, which was in Scarborough. The first airfield I went to was Sywell, [Northamptonshire] that's where the Tiger Moths were and we had three months there. After that we went to SFTS [Service Flying Training School] and flew with Blenheims, Oxfords and Blenheims, and then we were posted to our squadron. My first squadron was the Mosquito Squadron, which I didn't want to join because I'd never heard of the Mosquitos. The very first Mosquito Squadron to be formed and I wanted to go on Blenheims, just as well I did, they made me go. A lovely aircraft, wooden aircraft.

I think I had quite good night vision and the first squadron were scheduled to form the night fighters, not the bombers, the night fighters. So I was posted with the Night Fighter Squadron, 157 Squadron, in a place called Sywell. It was very, very exciting when these things took off. The stalling speed was 90 miles per hour, 80–90 miles an hour, so you took off at 120, which was very fast. And I was 18 years old. I loved it, loved it. It took some getting used to. Once you had mastered the aircraft there was no aircraft like it. Except the Spitfire.

The height of the Blitz had passed by then, but there were still occasional bombers coming over and we were night fighters. We had to intercept those [German] night fighters. We had radar, you had an observer with you of course, and a radar set, and you used to follow

the observer's directions who took you onto the aircraft as you could see it. And then you opened fire and hoped [the other pilot] didn't see you first. It was all night flying, which was very demanding, on a pitch black night you had no horizon, all instinct flying the whole time. Then, of course, once you fired your guns everybody's finished, whether you hit them or not. Because once you fired your guns the backflash from the guns ruins your night vision. And everything becomes pitch black. You'd wait another two or three minutes. By that time [the other pilot] had scarpered. Sometimes you didn't know whether you had hit him or not, I knew I hit one, I know that I saw bits coming off.

I did a tour for a year night flying. And then I was posted to a photographic reconnaissance unit [PRU]. Still in Mosquitos, but that was in Burma so I had to go from here to Burma and that was very dicey. I didn't like that. In night flying, if you're shot down, you're shot over the North Sea or in this country, but in PRU, if you're shot down you're shot in the middle of the jungle in Burma. It was very exciting. But I had two very good navigators both in night fighters and in PRU. So they always told me where I was. It was quite exciting. PRU was very exciting because you're going backwards and forwards over a target, and of course any ack-ack that got onto us knew you were coming back and just waited, and going back again you were going through it all. That's when there was ack-ack. Of course a lot of the time there wasn't any ack-ack but Rangoon was a hot spot.

War is hellish. It wasn't actually. Some parts you enjoyed, but some parts you were shit scared. What's best, mind you, when you're scared you're far more up to it, you know your reactions are far quicker.

After the war I joined the Ordnance Survey, which was very good, and I was posted at Glasgow, which was even better because it was in Scotland, and where 602 Squadron were based. They were a squadron of Spitfires, they flew from Abbotsinch. So I applied to fly with them and I flew with them for about 10 years. It's funny that, I was commissioned in the Air Force but when I joined the Auxiliaries I had to revert back to being Sergeant. There were no commissioned vacancies so I had to work my way up again. But then eventually I became Flight Commander there at 602 Squadron. It was very, very good. You worked during the week but most of your weekends, Saturdays and Sundays, were spent flying. The wife didn't like it very much. I mean, I couldn't take her shopping! She was on her own most of the time. They paid you, of course, I mean Aberdonians are like that!

All the pilots I spoke to thought that Spitfires were great and very light. I had never flown one before, but, because I flew Mosquitos during the war and they were also light, they were made of wood, so I thought I knew what to expect. I think the Mosquito was faster than the Spitfire, but not nearly as manoeuvrable. I mean the Spitfire, you'd have to ask the Germans how they felt about it. I think it could outturn most of the aircraft.

I wouldn't say it was a dream come true getting to fly Spitfires. I was glad, mind you. I loved the Mosquitos. You can't fly a thing for four or five years and just transfer. But I, shall we say, yes, it became a dream come true because I got to love the Spitfire, put it that way. You could do things in a Spitfire you couldn't do with a Mosquito. I enjoyed them both. I think I preferred the Spitfire, yes.

You see, you were by yourself. In the Mosquito you had an observer. I was 18 or 19 flying the Mosquito and the observer was 26. He was married, and what always got on your mind was if you got it wrong and anything happened to him, he has a wife and kids. With a Spitfire, anything happens to you and it's your own problem. That's the main difference though. In a Spitfire you're by yourself and in a Mosquito you have to think of somebody else.

If you were flying the Mosquito you had two engines, so you've no swing on take-off. It was balanced. In a Spitfire there's one engine and torque going one way. It scares the shit out of you. The first time you take off you don't know where you're going, the swing is terrific, you have to correct it right away. The second time, once you understand it, it's OK. But once in the air there is no comparison between planes. The Spitfire was, I think, *the* plane. The aerodynamics of it was perfect. And aerobatics – you enjoyed doing aerobatics. You wanted to do it. I think the Spitfire has got a place in my heart, which the Mosquito hasn't. I took two tours in the Mosquito, I must admit. Night fighters and PRU, but I still prefer the Spitfire.

In the 602 Squadron you had no special aircraft, you just – I think it was 12 Spitfires – you just flew the one that was allocated to you. I think I flew one more than most but it was just the luck of the draw. You just signed, one came in and landed, the pilot got out, somebody else took it out, that's it.

The first crash I had in a Spitfire, I managed to land her. [This was on 31st October 1948 in LA222, RAI-M.] It was just a normal day. We took off in formation I think, or two of us took off in formation. And over Glenboig [North Lanarkshire] the engine just started spluttering really, really, badly. And then suddenly it

Jim Johnston at Tangmere, 1953.

packed in altogether. It was a matter of bailing out or staying with the aircraft, and it wasn't a highly occupied area mind you, but it didn't worry me, mind. My own safety was the most important, the more you think of it, but it did flash over your mind, there was occasional houses, now I had read reports that they were not too bad when we crash landed. Now all-metal aircraft – a wooden aircraft would have been different – but it was all-metal, so I just stayed with it and picked a field, any field, there was no power left; you just had to pick a field and land it. And of course there were three hillocks in that field. Three small hillocks and I hit the top of every bloody one of them. I was never scratched, which I must admit was due to the Spitfire. A very, very sturdy aircraft. If that had been the Mosquito it would have been matchwood.

I don't know the cause of the crash, just engine failure. It was running very rough. Not when it took off, but afterwards it was running very rough. And it was engine failure. I'm not sure of the technicalities. I didn't worry about it much at the time.

When I got out and looked at it it was not too bad. I did a wheels-up landing. You never do a free-nose-down landing if you don't know the territory because you can go on your nose like with a wee bump, you always land with your wheels up, and I don't think it even bounced once. It was salvageable, the aircraft, there wasn't much damage done. The propeller was bent of course. The guns were OK. The bodywork was scratched, but not too bad. They were very sturdy the Spitfires, they were all metal. Scary mind you. No, I wouldn't say scary, you were too excited to be scared. When the engine starts to go you think 'Oh my God', but then you are too busy doing things to worry about it. Then when you land you climb out, wipe the sweat off your brow and that's it.

The second time I crashed was in LA198. We were at Summer Camp in Horsham St. Faith [Norfolk] in July 1949. Much the same thing happened, engine failure again. I managed to ground-loop the aircraft to avoid some kind of obstruction and landed safely. The aeroplane was a complete write off. I think it's a gate guardian at some airfield, but I'm not sure. I know it's still in existence, but at which airfield I couldn't tell you. There was no worry about it; there was a surplus of Spitfires so it wasn't really troubling very much. You got a replacement next day because the war had just ended and all the Spitfires were lying about.

I think it is a great thing to preserve this Spitfire. I mean after all, where would the country be if it wasn't for the Battle of Britain? The Spitfire won the Battle of Britain. I think it is right that we should look back on these events. Yes, and maybe some more. You never know. I mean, I don't think there would be the same kind of war. No, it's history, I think it should be kept.

						TIGER MOTH :-	
		UNIT :- 602 Sqdn. R. Aux. A.F.					
		DATE :- 1/7/49					
o/c SQUADRON		SIGNATURE :- J. O. Johnston					
JULY	2	HARVARD	584	SELF	P° SCOTT	I. F.	
JULY	16	SPITFIRE	F	SELF		BASE TO MIDDLETON S? GEO	
JULY	17	SPITFIRE	F	SELF		MIDDLETON TO FINNINGLEY	
JULY	19	SPITFIRE	F	SELF		FINNINGLEY TO HORSHAM	
JULY	20	SPITFIRE	N	SELF		FORMATION	
JULY	21	SPITFIRE	F	SELF		u/c u/s RETURNED TO BASE	
JULY	22	SPITFIRE	G	SELF		ENGINE TROUBLE, PRANGED ON	
			LA198			DID NOT FLY AGAIN	
				GRAND TOTAL [Cols. (1) to (10)]		TOTALS CARRIED FORWARD	

I joined up in 1941 but, three or four years prior to that, I had noticed an [Avro] 504K crash land at Netherton Farm at Bridge of Allan. And I cycled down there and had a look over it and it looked [a] pretty monstrous affair to me. Now, following that, I had noticed Alan Cobham's [Flying] Circus at a place called Kippen in Stirlingshire and was quite fascinated by the way they were carrying on with the aircraft. I thought they were out of control and it turned out they were actually doing a spin. You know, deliberately doing a spin and pulling out at 1,000 feet. I thought that was fantastic. So, a friend of mine, Johnny McArthur said to me, 'You fancy it, I fancy it. Do you think we should go along, and see what the score is?'. I said, fair enough, we'd do that. So we finished up going along to Hanover Street, Edinburgh, and after our four-day medical and aptitude test, it was decided that I'd be offered training as a pilot and Johnny was offered training as a navigator. And we thought, well that was great. He says to me, he says, 'Sandy, if you could be a pilot and I'll be a navigator and that's it'. Well that was the start of it.

However, my call up took place much, much sooner than his, and I was called up and went down to London. From there to ITW [Initial Training Wing] at Babbacombe in Devon and from there to America. And the first place we hit in America was a place called Albany in Georgia, and we were possibly there for about less than a week, and then a batch of us were dispatched to a place called Dara Aerotech where we became aviation cadets. We were incorporated into the American Air Corps. We wore their dress, we were no longer wearing the Air Force uniform because they weren't in the war at the particular time, we were just wearing the khaki slacks and the khaki shirts. My instructor down there was an old bush pilot by the name of Pete Lolla, and it was absolutely fantastic. Like everybody else, I thought it would never last and then after about a fortnight we realized we were on the course. We were definitely lasting and from then on it was the Air Corps the whole time.

I completed my training in America and came back to this country and was sent to 53 Operational Training Unit South Wales where I was introduced to the Spitfire 1. I was sent off solo and that sort of thing, and completed the OTU there in Spit 1s and 2s. And then I was sent to North Weald to be introduced to a Spit 5 and the next thing, I was on my way to North Africa by boat. We joined 154 Squadron in Lentini, Sicily, and then moved from Lentini up to Milazzo on the north tip of Sicily. 322 Wing, five squadrons and covered the Salerno show. And after Salerno, moved from there to a placed called Gioia del Colle, all in Spit 9s by this time. Next thing was, we were sent down to Ramat David in Palestine for new equipment. We got brand new machines down there and nobody knew exactly where we were going. But we finished up in Syria, with half the ground staff in Turkey over the border, because we were four miles from Turkey's border. We were there until Christmas 1943 and then, come round about January or February, we moved back down to Ramat David and back round up into Corsica.

We did a few shows on the Italian mainland from Corsica, and then we moved up to a place called Beretta, which is about three or four miles south of Bastia, and got knocked out thoroughly one night by 88s. Absolutely eliminated. The reason being that a Liberator on the Ploesti raid had lost an engine and came swinging on down there instead of going home, and crash-landed right on our strip at Beretta. Of course, they just put a half-track out and a wire rope pulled the whole thing to the end of the strip, and the first salvo of anti-personnel, from the JU88s, down about 1000 feet, hit right across the head, at the top of the Liberator, like a fantastic torch, to the end of the runway. And they went up and down there at will. Absolutely at will. They couldn't put two aircraft in the air the following day but by lunchtime the ferry pilots had replaced practically all. Every cook and butcher on that wing [that was Five Squad], every pilot, everyone walked up and down that runway two or three times, picking up shrapnel. The first guy to make a take off was Group Captain Hugo. He burst a tyre and turned over. However, he was OK, so we did the runway up and down again], pulling out shrapnel.

Now the next thing was, to get back in groove again, because we were all equipped from the afternoon on. 'Axis Sal' [the Axis Forces [Germany and Italy] propagandist], came on the radio that particular night and said, 'Well all you guys at Beretta know all about it now', and, immediately there was a panic on and we departed Beretta within two hours and went on to Calvi on the other side of Corsica. Now the significant thing about that trip was that the two Beaufighters, night fighters from Bastia, had followed the bomber stream. They had used the bomber stream onto a place called Montélimar, half way up France. And the following day two squadrons of American Lightnings went in and carved the whole lot up. And the significance of it is that later on in the war we actually arrived at Montélimar, and every blast made had JU88s burned out, phenomenal. Anyway, so that puts us into Calvi and we did a few shows at Calvi and went across to France and we were the first Spits in the South of France.

The CO said to me, 'Right, take three clapped-outs [aeroplanes that were to be scrapped], and dump them at Cagliari, down Sardinia and then make your way to Heliopolis'. We thought we were in for the Normandy show, but he said, 'No, just make your way to

Heliopolis'. So we went down to Heliopolis and attended the gunnery school down there and it turned out that it was right out in the sticks and that every joker on this unit was tour expired [when a pilot's tour of duty had ended and he had done ground duty, he was required to refresh his skills before flying again]. Bomber crews, you know, navigators, gunners what have you.

Then I came back to this country, joined 234 Squadron and within a short time on Mustangs the CO suggested that I might fancy going down to a place called Upavon [Wiltshire], under the jurisdiction of Group Captain Britain. And it was Group Captain Britain's idea to take all operational pilots and train them as instructors. First time that had ever happened. Well, I graduated from that place and went from there

Alex Bowman in Spitfire F.22, 1950.

to number 3FTS down in Feltwell as an instructor. Then I completed tours in the Air Force right up until 1950 as an instructor at Feltwell and then when they said to me, 'Right, you have a eight-year reserve commitment', it was then that I suggested why don't I join 602? That was when I joined it.

I can remember the first day in a Spitfire as if it was yesterday. It was a grim day and there was a recall that went out. You know when you go to an Operational Training Unit you first of all become conversant with the pilot's logbook. You got to know that perfectly, then somebody comes out and says to you, 'Right, OK, close your eyes. Where is this, that and the next thing?' When he thinks you know, you go out the first time in it. When he is confident that you're confident enough he lets you go. Of course I taxied round into position because you've got to get there in a pretty desperate hurry as they warm up very, very rapidly. And I did not get the recall, that was the first blunder, I did not get the recall. So I got off and practically closed down to three or 400 feet and came skittering back round and landed again, successfully, and got a rocket because the plug had come undone. My radio plug had come undone. That's why I couldn't get the recall. So that was the start.

Every pilot feels excited about flying a Spitfire for the first time, particularly a Spit 1, because it's such a beautiful aircraft, absolutely beautiful aircraft. I mean you got to the stage where you could roll with your pinkie, just the normal speed, but you could roll it with your pinkie. It was such a beautiful aircraft to fly. It was

never designed to be on the ground, you understand, because of all sorts of problems with people sort of bending props and what have you. And a crosswind, you know, even taxiing in a cross wind if you burned out the brake, you'd be all over the place. But I was successful and fortunate in that respect, thoroughly enjoyed it, I loved every minute of it.

The thing that was always significant to me was once you get into a Spit and really roped in, anything you want to do, you do. You don't have to think about it. They were wonderful machines to fly. Strictly defensive of course, they weren't very good offensively. I'm telling you about the Spit 1s, 2s and even the 5s. By the time you get onto the 9s, the 8s and 9s, you're getting heavier and heavier, because you've moved onto cannon from guns, you've moved onto cannon. The aircraft's got a four-bladed prop now, and it's become heavier and heavier and it's not the six ton job you were flying at OTU. But it's still a lovely aircraft. Might be operating with, well I think the Merlin, that was the engine that used to be in them. And they were really magnificent, they were really, really dependable for you. Once you were in there it was like a part of you. Then much later on, you go onto 21, 22, 14s, what have you, you have a five-bladed prop, and they were real brutes, real brutes. I mean a Spit these days was a 9, a 90-gallon tank up the front and to get to wherever you were going, it was sometimes necessary to have a 30-gallon jettison right below the belly. And then it went from a 30-, it went to a 90-gallon jettison tank.

And some of them had a 120-gallon jettison tank.

You know, you can just imagine how the aircraft behaved under these conditions. At the Salerno show, for instance, you always carried a minimum of 30 gallons. And as you were in the territory, if there was anything operational at all, everybody jettisoned their tanks, that put the aircraft clean and you were sitting full up. And once again, even at that you could only stay over there maybe, about 20, 25 minutes. And when you were coming out of somewhere, every pilot that was ever on the show always said the same thing because all the Air Sea Rescue launches and all the rest of it, all these guys used to hover above Stromboli. So when you were coming back from Salerno, there was nothing at all but sea, but you knew Stromboli. So every pilot that was ever on the Salerno show, always said the same thing, 'Halle-bloody-lujah, Stromboli', because you knew if you had to get out then you were home. There was always somebody there for you.

I was very lucky to have very good vision. We had a lecture from a professor in the Glasgow University, and he indicated that 10 people could have 20-20 vision but that does not necessarily mean that number one has the same vision as number 10. He says when you are in the flying game, if you're going to be any good at all, you have to have better than 20-20 vision. And, touch wood, I always was. I mean all through my career, they always said above average night vision and day vision. And I was always aware that I had exceptional day vision. You know, in 602 I had things long pinned before anyone else, which makes a fantastic difference.

Well, as I indicated earlier on, I had a commitment,

an eight-year commitment, to the Reserves. The lad that mentioned this to me, I said, 'What does that mean?' He says, 'It means that, anywhere you go, you've got to advise us when you're going to be back and all the rest of it'. So, that precluded me from going to Canada. I asked, 'What sort of flying, you know, keep your hand in?', he said, 'Oh yes, you will be able to get some Tiger time, up at Scone'. I said, 'Surely if we have to carry on for another eight years in the Reserve, would it not better in a fighter squad, there is a 602 Squadron up there?'. He says, 'Well, if you could, that is fair enough with us', but I did, I joined 602.

Marcus Robinson was the CO at the time. When I went into see him, he said, 'Well, we're pretty full up, but I've been speaking to young Maxwell up there (who happened to have had the same instructor at Upavon, the Instructor Flying Training School, as me), and he said that you would be a real asset to the squad'. I said, 'I think I would, Sir, I'm a pilot attack instructor, I'm a qualified flying instructor and I'm operational'. He said 'Yeah, OK', and that was it.

Of course, 602 Squadron was a flying club, an absolute flying club. It was incidental that Marcus Robinson was the CO at the time. He was a 1936 pilot and to Marcus it was just an Elite Flying Corp, as far as he was concerned. You used to see him, and he'd say, 'I think we'll pop on down to down south,' you know, down to Horsham or something like that. He'd take out a little diary, with a little map of Britain in it and he'd say, 'I think 190 should get us there. OK, climb in', and we all did. Then along came Group Captain Stephen, a veteran of the Battle of Britain and a very, very close friend of Max Aitken [Lord Beaverbrook], and the whole thing took on an entirely different complexion. He was a fighter and although he was over the hill himself and told you straight, that was Steve, he was over the hill himself but he could get things done. There was nothing that 602 required that they didn't get because if he couldn't get it one way, other channels that he knew could get it. Fantastic CO.

I did not approve of the flying club approach, not at all. I mean anybody that was in 602, the Battle of Britain men, like George Pinkerton, these characters they knew it was a flying club. They were sticking their neck out, you know, during the war, but after the war… It was irritating because Marcus was one of those guys, you know, he'd toss a coin, 'I'm thinking about flying today'. Casual, very casual and all that sort of thing. Ask any pilot, it wasn't really until Steve arrived that the thing became a fighter squadron. And he really, really worked at it and every CO that followed him worked flat out to do it as well. 'Cause you see, it was a part-time affair, that's how it was when Marcus was the CO, it was a part-time affair. Therefore, it was a flying club, but when you see the regular COs they were committed to their career and it was a different ball game then, they were whipping them into shape.

Well the Spitfire that Glasgow has acquired, the Spit 21, you were onto an entirely different ball game from the previous 9, 8, 16 and 18s. Here we have a Griffon engine, not a Merlin, a Griffon engine with a five-bladed prop, which would kill you as soon as look at you. And many, many pilots hated the sight of them. On take off for a start, if you throttled, if you gave it too much power too early it would turn off, right off the runway at right angles. Right angles right off the runway. Fortunately we didn't lose, well, we lost an aircraft now and then, you know in mud and what have you, but never actually a write-off. But lots of guys, on a balked landing gave coal, gave it throttle and just went straight and turned it on its back, the aircraft turned on the prop.

Dozens of them bought it on a balked landing, so you were always transferring people. It was very easy to say, 'Oh, you're a Spitfire pilot, there is a 21, get into it.' It wasn't as easy as that. There are a few warnings that have to be given to jokers that were transferring from a four-blader to a five-blader, particularly the Griffon. Great engine, great machine when it is in the air, marvellous.

A rare photograph of LA198 at Abbotsinch in 1949.

(Formerly of Rolls Royce, Malcolm was associated with the Griffons from 1965 until he retired at the end of March 1999.)

The twinning of Spitfires with Merlins and Griffons was due to circumstance really. Rolls Royce decided that a bigger engine than the Rolls Royce Kestrel was necessary, and the government at the time wouldn't fund the development of that engine, so they went ahead as a private venture, and so simultaneously we were working on Vickers Supermarine and we were looking at an aircraft to meet a Ministry Spec, and the Merlin, as it became, was exactly the right size of engine on the aircraft, hence the link up between the Merlin and the Spitfire.

The Merlin was very successful and very timely too, with the arrival of the Second World War. It was a match for the German aircraft of the period. There was obviously a lot of development work went into the Merlin, particularly during the Battle of Britain and the immediate aftermath, and there was a case of Britain and Germany leapfrogging each other technologically and the developments in the Merlin were very instrumental in keeping the Spitfire ahead of the German technology at the time.

The Merlin reached the end of its usefulness as far as the Spitfire was concerned really because it was becoming more and more difficult to develop the power level of the Merlin. Although, having said that, after the war a Merlin was running at power levels way beyond what we could achieve during the war, but there were risks to running at high powers, engine failures, etc. If a larger engine could be installed in the Spitfire then that would extend the useful life of the aircraft and the Griffon happened to be the engine that filled that role.

The Griffon is a pretty old engine in Rolls Royce terms, it actually first saw the light of day in 1933. It was more or less a de-tuned Schneider trophy R-Engine, the engine that won the Schneider trophy for Britain. The R-Engine in turn was based on the Buzzard, which was a late 1920s V12 engine. Unfortunately, for various reasons the Griffon of 1933 was sidelined, and work went ahead on the PV12 which became the Merlin. So it wasn't until 1938 that the idea of the Griffon was resurrected and there was a lot of radical redesign done, because the idea of putting a Griffon into a Spitfire had occurred to the senior designers in the company. One of the main redesigns was to make it shorter because the engines are a pretty long piece of machinery.

In 1939 a Griffon was installed in a Spitfire to make sure that it would fit the available space, and there were one or two external units that would have stuck out through the cowling. They were all redesigned to make sure that it fitted and in 1941 the Spitfire flew with the Griffon installed, the one and only Spitfire 4. The Air Ministry decided that the Griffon should go into the Firefly. I should perhaps explain that there were three candidates for the Griffon at that time, one was the

Beaufighter, one was the Fairey Firefly, and the last one was the Spitfire. The Air Ministry decided that priority should be given to the Fairey Firefly, so again the Griffon was sidelined as a Spitfire engine until the appearance of the Focke-Wulf 190 which was causing all sorts of problems, both at high level and at low level. The development work that had been done particularly on superchargers for Merlins had resulted in aircraft like the Spitfire 9 which could handle the Focke-Wulf 190 at altitude but not at low level, so there was a trial fly-off done in late 1940 between the one and only Spitfire Mark 4, a Hawker Typhoon, and a captured Focke-Wulf 190, and that established quite clearly that the Spitfire 4 with the Griffon engine was more than a match at low

level for the Focke-Wulf 190. So the Air Ministry decided that there was an immediate requirement to produce Griffon-powered Spitfires and taking the Spitfire Mark 8 and taking out the Merlin and fitting the Griffon achieved that. Obviously it wasn't quite as simple as that, but fortunately all of the preliminary work had been done in 1939 to shoehorn a Griffon into the Spitfire.

I should say that there isn't an awful lot of difference in size between a Merlin and Griffon. The Griffon's frontal area for instance is only five per cent bigger than a Merlin, and at that time it was only three inches longer, so as an interim measure the Spitfire Mark 8 was

Making Merlin engines at Rolls Royce Hillington.

fitted with the Griffon and entered service as Spitfire Mark 12, that was in 1942. There was no real change in the Griffon-powered Spitfire fleet until 1944, when Spitfire 14 came along, and that was followed late 1944 by Spitfire Mark 21, which was effectively the redesigned Spitfire to suit the Griffon, that the Spitfire 12 had filled the space for, so that's the sort of history of the Merlin and the Griffon.

The Merlin continued to be fitted into Spitfires. Spitfire 9 was probably one of the most important of the Spitfire versions. It stayed in production for quite some time. Spitfire 16 was the final mark of the Spitfire that was fitted with the Merlin. So they ran in parallel. There were an awful lot more Merlins for the Spitfires built than the Griffon. As you can imagine, the pressure was on the Battle of Britain and subsequent years 1941/42. Most of the emphasis was on building Spitfires, most of which I think were probably Spitfire 9s, with small numbers of Griffon-powered Spitfires to meet the need.

The main advantage of the Griffon over the Merlin was power, for instance the Spitfire Mark 1 as it was pre-war, in the early days of the Battle of Britain, was powered by a Merlin 1, a Merlin 2 or a Merlin 3. They were all pretty much of a muchness with regard to power levels. They gave the aircraft 890 brake horsepower for take off and something like 1030 brake horsepower at the maximum power height, which was 16,250 feet. A Spitfire 21 with the Griffon 61, it had 1540 brake horsepower available for take off. That was only because the aircraft didn't need more power at sea level to take off. The engine could provide 1935 brake horsepower at sea level at maximum boost, and 2035 brake horsepower at 21,000 feet, which was where most of the fighting by that time of the war had been done, so it was really a matter of power levels. The Griffon never actually achieved the sort of specific power levels that the Merlin was capable of, one of the reasons being that the Griffon's maximum RPM is 2750 and the Merlin's is 3000, so the Merlin could always produce that wee bit extra in specific power.

The external dimensional package was very similar, but the Griffon has an engine that is very much bigger in capacity, it's 36.7 litres compared to 27, so it had a lot more capability.

The Griffon 61, which was the power plant for the Spitfire 21, could develop up to 2035 brake horsepower at its maximum power altitude. The Griffon, in common with any supercharged engine, has fuel air mixture passing through the supercharger. It gets heated up because it is being compressed and, if that fuel air mixture is at too high a temperature when it goes into the cylinder, instead of burning as the spark ignites, you get an explosive combustion. It's the same thing as pinking in your car, but in an engine the size of the Griffon or the Merlin if you do nothing about that detonation it can melt a piston in seconds because you have one cylinder that's misbehaving and 11 other cylinders that's keeping it going, so you have to avoid the possibility of detonation. That's partly done by richening the mixture but it is also done by limiting the boost that's produced by the supercharger. Griffon 61 had a maximum operating boost pressure, 18lbs. The air going into the cylinders was at a pressure 18lbs per square inch higher than atmospheric, and all the pilot had to do was open the throttle fully and he would get 18lbs boost. When I say the pilot fully opens the throttle through his lever, the engine has an automatic boost control unit which, to prevent detonation, would partially close or prevent the engine throttle from opening fully. So when at sea level the engine is partially throttled, producing its 18lbs boost and hence 1935 brake horsepower, as the altitude increases the engine throttle progressively opens until at what we call the full throttle height it is fully open and the engine is developing the full power that it is capable of doing, which in the case of the Griffon 61 is 2035.

The Griffon is a V12 engine of 36.7 litres capacity whereas the Merlin, although it's also a V12, only has 27 litres capacity. The design of the Griffon is such that it doesn't occupy much more space than the Merlin, but because it has the extra cylinder capacity it is capable of theoretically developing more power and that was one of the original reasons for suggesting that the Griffon should be installed in the Spitfire because it was a similar-sized power plant package to the Merlin but had the greater power package.

The usefulness of the Spitfire had more or less gone by 1948 with the advent of the gas turbine, so that there was no incentive to keep developing the Merlin as a military engine, but of course it carried on after the war as a very successful commercial engine in aircraft like the DC4M Argonaut, etc. Although it wasn't developed as a

military engine, it did carry on as a commercial enterprise. The Griffon with the demise of the Spitfire was fortunate in that it fitted the bill for the post-war development of the Lancaster, which became the Shackleton AEW. That wasn't originally an early warning aeroplane, it was maritime reconnaissance but stayed in service for a long, long, time and eventually finished up as an airborne early warning aircraft. In terms of power, the engine that was in the Shackleton was the most powerful of all the Griffons at low level, producing 2450 brake horsepower which is way beyond anything that the Spitfire engines produced, but it ran out of steam and altitude because the designs were low-level. That was in service until 1980.

In 1939, when it was realized that the war was going to come and because of the importance of the Merlin to the RAF (after all it was installed in both the Spitfire and in larger numbers in the Hurricane), the decision was made to build shadow factories throughout Britain. One of those was in Hillington, so there has been Rolls Royce presence in the Glasgow area since then. It gradually expanded beyond Hillington in other sites like Cardonald, and in the early '50s the East Kilbride site was opened, mainly to build Avon Engines for the Korean War, and that itself spawned other factories in Blantyre and Larkhall, and eventually the engineering team moved to the Hamilton factory. Over recent years these smaller sites have all been closed and we now have Hillington and East Kilbride as the Rolls Royce presence in Scotland.

Airspeed A.S.10 Oxford:	British three-seat, twin-engine, monoplane advanced trainer. First flew in 1937 and remained in service until 1954/55.
Avro 504:	British two-seat, single-engine, biplane elementary trainer. Adopted by the RAF after the First World War as a trainer aircraft, it remained in production until 1937.
Avro Lancaster:	British seven-seat, four-engine, monoplane heavy bomber. First flew in 1941.
Bristol Beaufighter:	British two-seat, twin-engine, monoplane night/long range fighter /bomber.
Bristol Blenheim:	British two-seat, twin-engine, monoplane long range/night fighter /bomber.
Consolidated B-24 Liberator:	American seven-seat, four-engine, monoplane heavy bomber. First flew in 1940.
Consolidated PBY-1 > PBY- 6A Catalina:	American seven-/nine-seat, twin-engine, monoplane long range maritime reconnaissance amphibian flying boat. First flew in 1935 and continued in use well after the end of the Second World War.
De Havilland DH 9/19A:	British two-seat, single-engine, biplane day bomber. First entered RAF service in 1918 and remained in use until 1931.
De Havilland Mosquito:	British two-seat, twin-engine, monoplane night fighter/fighter bomber. First flew in 1940.
De Havilland Moth/Tiger Moth:	British two-seat, single-engine, biplane initial trainer. First flew in 1925.
De Havilland Vampire:	British single-seat, single-engine turbojet interceptor fighter. Britain's second jet fighter design.
Defiant (Boulton Paul Defiant):	British two-seat, single engine, monoplane night fighter. First flew in 1937. Fitted with power-driven turret in rear fuselage.
Dornier DO17:	German three-/four-seat, twin-engine, monoplane medium bomber (long-range reconnaissance). Initially flew as a six-passenger commercial aircraft in 1934.
Fairey Fawn:	British two-seat, single-engine, biplane day bomber. First flew in 1923, withdrawn from operational duties in 1926, with supplementary service until 1929.
Focke-Wulf 190:	German single-seat, single engine, monoplane fighter and ground attack. First flew June 1939.
Gloster Gauntlet:	British single-seat, single-engine, biplane fighter. Entered RAF service in 1935, subsequently withdrawn from operational service early in the Second World War.
Gloster Gladiator:	British single-seat, single-engine, biplane interceptor fighter. First flew in 1934.
Gloster Meteor:	British single-seat, twin-engine turbojet interceptor fighter. Britain's first jet fighter design, flew for the first time in 1943.
Handley Page Hampden:	British four-seat, twin-engine, monoplane medium bomber. First flew in 1936.
Hawker Hart:	British two-seat, single-engine, biplane day bomber. Entered RAF service in 1930 and subsequently was removed from operational service to become an RAF trainer aircraft in 1936.
Hawker Hector:	British two-seat, single-engine, biplane Army Co-operation aircraft. In service from 1937 to late 1940.
Hawker Hind:	British two-seat, single-engine, biplane light bomber. Entered RAF service in 1935, subsequently withdrawn from operational service in 1939.

Hawker Hurricane:	British single-seat, single-engine, monoplane fighter and fighter bomber. First flew in 1935.
Hawker Tempest:	British single-seat, single-engine, monoplane interceptor and fighter bomber. First flew in 1942. Was to become Britain's mainstay in the defence against Germany's flying bomb – the V1.
Hawker Typhoon:	British single-seat, single-engine, monoplane fighter bomber. First flew in 1940.
Hawker/BAe Harrier:	British single-seat, single vectored-thrust turbofan, ground-attack aircraft. First flew in 1966.
Heinkel HE 111:	German four-seat, twin-engine, monoplane medium bomber. Initially demonstrated as a 10-passenger commercial aircraft in 1936.
JU 88 (Junkers JU 88):	German three-/four-seat, twin-engine, monoplane night fighter/light bomber. First flew in 1936.
Junkers JU 87 (Stuka):	German two-seat, single-engine, monoplane dive bomber. First flew in 1935.
Lockheed P-38 Lightning:	American single-seat, twin-engine monoplane fighter. First flew in 1939.
Messerschmitt BF 109:	German single-seat, single-engine, monoplane fighter. First flew in 1935.
Messerschmitt ME 110:	German two-seat, twin-engine, monoplane long range day and escort fighter. First flew in 1936.
North American Harvard:	American two-seat, single-engine, monoplane advanced trainer. First flew in 1937.
North American P-51 Mustang:	American single-seat, single-engine, monoplane long-range fighter. First flew in 1940.
Panavia Tornado GR1/GR4:	Italy, Germany and Great Britain partnership. A two-seat, twin-engine turbofan medium range, low-level supersonic counter-air strike aircraft. First flew in 1974. Also F3, an air defence variant.
Saro London:	British six-seat, twin-engine, biplane general purpose coastal reconnaissance flying boat. First flew in 1934, withdrawn from operational service in 1941.
V1 'Flying Bomb':	German un-piloted, single ram-jet, flying bomb.
V2: Rocket:	German un-piloted, long range ballistic missile.
Vickers Armstrong Wellington:	British six-seat, twin-engine, monoplane long-range bomber. First flew in 1936. Used Barnes Wallace's geodetic construction.
'Wee Bee':	Very small, single-seat light aircraft. Beardmore's winning entry in the Air Ministry's light aircraft design competition in the 1920s.
Westland Wapiti:	British two-seat, single-engine, biplane light bomber. Withdrawn from operational service in the early stages of the Second World War.

Chronology of Vickers Armstrong Supermarine Spitfire MK21. Serial LA198

21 September 1944	Aircraft completed at South Marston, Wiltshire. Test flown by Flt Lt Johnson, duration 25 minutes.
2 October 1944	Taken on charge at 33 MU Lyneham, delivered by Capt Hughes, ATA.
3 May 1945	Allocated to No. 1 Squadron.
4 October 1946	Placed in storage at 9 MU Cosford.
12 May 1947	Allocated to 602 (City of Glasgow) Squadron AAF.
25 October 1947	Damaged in a category 'A' flying accident.
11 May 1948	Repairs completed by 63 MU Carluke.
22 July 1949	Emergency landing at Horsham St Faith, owing to engine failure. Pilot Jim Johnston intentionally ground-looped aircraft. Category 'B' damage sustained.
9 August 1949	Dispatched to Vickers Armstrong, South Marston for repair.
21 July 1950	Repairs completed.
27 July 1950	Collected by 33 MU and placed in storage.
19 September 1951	Allocated to 3 Civilian Anti-Aircraft Co-operation Unit, Exeter.
19 November 1953	Returned to Vickers Armstrong for possible resale.
19 February 1954	Presented to 187 (City of Worcester) Squadron ATC. Given serial number 7118M.
1967–1968	Used in the *Battle of Britain* film.
1970	Restored and displayed as gate guardian at RAF Locking, Avon.
1973	Rolls Royce Griffon 61 engine removed for BBMF PR19.
March 1986	Moved to RAF Leuchars, Fife.
6 June 1986	Displayed as gate guardian at RAF Leuchars in dedication ceremony.
12 April 1989	Moved to RAF St Athan for storage.
1996	Moved to RAF Museum storage, Cardington.
1997	Gifted to the City of Glasgow.
4 March 1998	Delivered to the Museum of Flight, East Fortune, for restoration.
October 2002	Restoration completed.
July 2003	Returned to Glasgow in the year of the centenary of powered flight.

Castletown

Dyce

Tealing

Clydebank Grangemouth
Abbotsinch Turnhouse
Glasgow Slamannan Drem
  Glenboig
Prestwick Eaglesham
    Selkirk

Stranraer

Middleton St George

Scarborough

Warrington

Nottingham

Horsham St Faith
Sywell Norwich
    Feltwell

Fairwood Common North Weald
Cardiff South Marston Gerrard's Cross
  Bristol   London
    Upavon Middle Wallop
    Goodwood Tangmere
    Westhampnett
Plymouth   Beachy Head
  Babbacombe

A formation of 602'S Spitfire 21s and 22s photographed over Loch Lomond, 7th November 1948. LA198 is third from the left.